A SHORT HISTORY OF THE ROMAN MASS

UWE MICHAEL LANG

A Short History of the Roman Mass

IGNATIUS PRESS SAN FRANCISCO

Cover art
The Last Supper
Gospel of the School of Reichenau, 10–11th century A.D.
Biblioteca Queriniana/Brescia/Italy

Cover design by Roxanne Mei Lum

ISBN 978-1-62164-697-6 (PB)
ISBN 978-1-64229-308-1 (eBook)
Library of Congress Control Number 2024942272
Printed in the United States of America ♾

CONTENTS

FOREWORD

by Christopher Carstens

The Catholic faithful can view the Mass from a variety of perspectives: ritually, symbolically, pastorally, rubrically, sociologically, artistically, spiritually, historically—to name more than a few. And each of these vantage points offers insight into the Mass' supernatural reality in our lives. Father Uwe Michael Lang provides the Church and the praying Catholic a great service by offering a reliable, concise, and insightful vision of the Western Church's greatest prayer in *A Short History of the Roman Mass*.

Reconstructing history, in any discipline, is no easy task. New textual evidence comes to light, even as once-held certainties are overturned. A noteworthy element in today's Roman Rite, for example, is the place of the so-called *Apostolic Tradition*, a document once thought to be authored by Saint Hippolytus, in Rome, in the early third century. The *Apostolic Tradition* formed the basis of several current liturgical rites, including the second Eucharistic Prayer and aspects of the Order of Christian Initiation of Adults. But recent findings have called into doubt substantial aspects of the document, such as its author, its provenance, and its substance. How should we understand today's liturgy in light of these historical findings?

Similarly, a common historical narrative following fast on the close of the Second Vatican Council told a story of early and vibrant liturgical development, followed by early medieval corruption, late medieval decline, and modern stagnation—followed by a glorious rebirth with the Second Vatican Council. But more recent findings suggest otherwise: even when and where elements of decay existed, the Church at such times also evidenced a vibrant liturgical life. What does such a corrected narrative mean for us today?

Furthermore, consider that much modern commentary depicts a misguided liturgical overhaul of the rite of the Mass as it has been handed down to us, largely unchanged for centuries. But a clearer vision sees not only substantial stability in essential parts—such as in the Canon of the Mass—but also variations according to time and place over time. The Mass is unchanged and yet it also changed. How is this so? How do we appreciate this complex dynamic of stability and adaptability through time?

Father Lang's *A Short History of the Roman Mass* clarifies liturgical questions such as these—and he does so in a well-written and accessible manner that even those of us without the benefit of years of historical study can appreciate. In fact, not only does the book present a fascinating story of the Mass, but Father Lang provides us with a glossary of terms to help us along our journey.

But aside from organizing the persons, events, and cultures of our Mass' history, Father Lang also looks at the larger picture of the liturgy and its life through the centuries. Why, after all, should we be concerned about the fourth-century *Barcelona Anaphora*, the eighth-century *Ordo Romanus*, or Johann Burchard's sixteenth-century Order of Mass? Catholics today—whether we know it or not, whether we are interested or not—owe our faith and its liturgical expression to ancestors such as these. The Roman Ritual family, like any family, has a history, and the fruits of this "family tree" are nourished from the organic soil and roots of the past. To appreciate the gift of the liturgy we have today, we must also value the past centuries from which the Mass has been cultivated.

Indeed, this organic metaphor for the liturgy—as a family tree—suggests a second reason we should appreciate our Mass' history. For today's liturgy is not the product of mere man-made artifice but is the product (or produce) of an organic growth over time: rather than a construct, the liturgy is an organism. And like any organism, it has been given life from sources outside and prior to itself. To pray today's collects well includes a familiarity with yesterday's sources. To see Christ at the Mass' elevations of the consecrated Host and the chalice is to possess, in part, the vision of this origin in the High Middle Ages. And to participate in the Universal Prayer of the Mass is to unite our voices with our ancestors as far back as Saint Justin Martyr in the second century. The liturgy lives—and we can receive its life more fruitfully when we are aware of its longevity.

Opinions about the ritual form of the Mass since the Second Vatican Council vary among practicing Catholics today. One line of thought sees today's Mass as too little related to its immediate pre-conciliar predecessor and considers this break a change for the better, an opportunity for a new Mass to speak to and represent a new age. Another angle agrees that the current form of the Mass has little in common with its past but considers the post-conciliar Mass a tragedy and terribly inferior to previous forms since it neglects the tradition from which it came.

Pope Benedict XVI knew of these threads of thought and considered that both—despite their diverse conclusions—make the same, basic error. Looking to the rocky reception of the Second Vatican Council generally, the Holy Father spoke of "warring hermeneutics", that is, conflicting interpretations of the council, the tradition, and the post-conciliar implementation. "The hermeneutic of discontinuity", he explains, "risks ending in a split between the pre-conciliar Church and the post-conciliar Church" (Message to Roman Curia, December 22, 2005). Such an interpretation does not see the council and its fruits—including the liturgy—in line with the treasure of tradition. Rather, it cuts the tree and its fruit away from the roots and soil from which they grew. Rather than this misguided hermeneutic of rupture, a "hermeneutic of reform" and renewal sees the Mass' organic growth from history and, looking onward and upward to the heavens, cultivates grace for men and women of our present age.

If Pope Benedict's evaluation of the council and its reception—as well as the conciliar Mass and its implementation—is correct, then a familiarity with our past is needed. As Father Lang writes, the "intense and often controversial debate on continuity and rupture in liturgical development" often takes place without sufficiently recognizing "the long and complex history of the Roman liturgy". For this reason alone, *A Short History of the Roman Mass* fills a need in our time.

In the end, whether the Mass and its reform is a source of debate and confusion, or an obligation, or, ideally, the means to encounter God, let Father Lang's *A Short History of the Roman Mass* help you to pray more intelligently and devoutly. The Mass is God's great gift to his people, not only throughout history but especially now. Accordingly, Father Lang offers this observation as his last word on the matter: "We may note the remarkable persistence of the Roman liturgical tradition, its rediscovery among the younger generations of Catholics, and the attraction it still holds for a wider cultural public." Whatever liturgical twists and turns have occurred over the years along the road to salvation, holiness—unto the glory of God—is our ultimate destination.

PREFACE

The Roman Rite is by far the most widely used among the liturgical rites of the Catholic Church. The form of Mass most people in the world are familiar with today has been shaped by the Apostolic See of Rome in contact and exchange with other local churches over the centuries. This book is intended as a short introduction to the development of the Roman Rite of Mass from its origins in early Christianity until the present day. Understanding this rich and complex history will help not only the clergy in their sacramental ministry but all the faithful in participating consciously and fruitfully in the liturgy of the Church.

The idea for this volume came as I was working on my recent monograph, which covers the history of the Roman Mass until the Tridentine reforms.[1] At the invitation of Christopher Carstens, I published a series of entries in *AB Insight*, the monthly newsletter of *Adoremus*, which I have revised so that they form a seamless narrative. Thanks are due to Cambridge University Press for the licence to reuse my material. With this book I hope to reach a broader readership; hence, I present the argument only in its essential outlines and use footnotes sparingly.

This work is dedicated in loving memory and gratitude to Pope Benedict XVI, who departed from this life

[1] Uwe Michael Lang, *The Roman Mass: From Early Christian Origins to Tridentine Reform* (Cambridge: Cambridge University Press, 2022).

on December 31, 2022. I am convinced that his epochal labors, which he pursued with intellectual courage, spiritual depth, and at great personal cost, have only begun to bear fruit and will prove his lasting legacy to the Church and the world.

1

The Last Supper

It would appear obvious to begin a history of the Eucharist with the Last Supper and its formative impact on early Christian liturgical practice. The Austrian Jesuit Josef Andreas Jungmann asserted in his classical work *Missarum sollemnia*: "The first Holy Mass was said on 'the same night in which he was betrayed' (1. Cor. 11:23)."[1] However, recent studies have presented a highly diverse picture of primitive Christianity, and the origins of the Eucharist have been subjected to radical questioning. Thus, the leading Anglican liturgical scholar Paul Bradshaw sees in the Institution narrative as recorded in the Synoptic Gospels a tradition superimposed on the original account of a simple meal.[2] On the other hand, many New Testament exegetes today are more confident about the essential historicity of the Last Supper tradition.[3]

[1] Josef A. Jungmann, *The Mass of the Roman Rite: Its Origins and Development (Missarum Sollemnia)*, trans. Francis A. Brunner, 2 vols. (New York: Benziger, 1951), 1:7.

[2] Paul Bradshaw, *Reconstructing Early Christian Worship* (Collegeville, MN: Liturgical Press, 2009), 3–19.

[3] For example, Brant Pitre, *Jesus and the Last Supper* (Grand Rapids, MI: Eerdmans, 2015); also Craig Blomberg, *Contagious Holiness: Jesus' Meals with Sinners* (Downers Grove, IL: InterVarsity Press, 2005), and Richard Bauckham, *Jesus and the Eyewitnesses: The Gospels as Eyewitness Testimony*, 2nd ed. (Grand Rapids, MI: Eerdmans, 2017).

A New Passover

While the meals Jesus held during his public ministry offer a broader context for the Last Supper,[4] there are several features that make it unique, above all its immediate proximity to his Passion. Unlike other meals recorded in the Gospels, this one is limited to the Twelve Apostles. The setting is not that of open table fellowship, but a private room that would have been provided by a wealthy patron. The words and actions of Jesus are embedded in this meal, but they stand out and transform it in an entirely unexpected way.

According to the Synoptic Gospels, Jesus celebrated the Last Supper with his disciples on the first day of unleavened bread in the evening (Mt 26:17, 20; Mk 14:12, 17; Lk 22:7, 14). Since Jews reckoned the day from sunset to sunset, this evening meal was held on the fourteenth day of the Jewish month Nisan, the date of the Passover feast, after the lambs had been sacrificed in the Temple in the afternoon. This day would be a Thursday, with the Crucifixion taking place on Friday, "the day before the sabbath" (Mk 15:42; cf. Mt 27:62; Lk 23:54), the fifteenth of Nisan. The Synoptic narratives thus present the Last Supper as a Passover meal.

The fourth Gospel presents a different chronology: while it agrees regarding the days of the week, it clearly implies that Jesus was crucified as the day of preparation for the Passover was drawing to its close (Jn 18:28, 39; 19:14). Significantly, Jesus died on the Cross at the time when the lambs were slaughtered in the Temple for the celebration of the Passover meal in the evening. The Last Supper was thus held on the evening before Passover, and it would not have

[4] See, for example, Eugene LaVerdiere, *Dining in the Kingdom of God: The Origin of the Eucharist according to Luke* (Chicago: Liturgical Training Publications, 1994).

been a Passover meal. Still, it would have been in close proximity to it, as explicitly stated in John 13:1, and thus bears many marks and meanings of the Passover. Unlike the Synoptics, John does not describe the meal itself, but focuses on Jesus' washing of the disciples' feet (13:2–11).

From the historian's point of view, it seems more likely that the Last Supper was not a Passover meal—a position supported by Joseph Ratzinger (Pope Benedict XVI) with reference to the work of the American biblical scholar John P. Meier.[5] Even so, at any Jewish formal meal, nothing was to be eaten without giving thanks to God and asking for his blessing. At the beginning of the Last Supper, some form of Jewish meal blessing (*berakah*) would have been said. We can also assume the ritual use of bread and wine, the latter being a particular sign of a festive occasion. However, what Jesus said and did at the occasion was unprecedented and cannot simply be derived from the Jewish ritual context. The actual words he spoke over the bread and over the cup of wine make them signs anticipating his redemptive Passion.

Jesus was fully aware that he was about to die, and he anticipated that he would not be able to celebrate the coming Passover according to Jewish tradition. Therefore, he gathered the Twelve, his innermost circle of disciples, for a special meal of farewell. While the reference to "this Passover" in Luke 22:15 could mean the meal Jesus was holding with the Twelve, it could also point to the new reality he was about to institute in anticipation of his Passion. The decisive moment of the Last Supper was not the customary Passover lamb (which even the Synoptics do not mention),

[5] Joseph Ratzinger [Pope Benedict XVI], *Jesus of Nazareth*, pt. 2, *Holy Week: From the Entrance into Jerusalem to the Resurrection*, trans. Philip J. Whitmore (San Francisco: Ignatius Press, 2011), 112–15, citing John R. Meier, *A Marginal Jew: Rethinking the Historical Jesus*, vol. 1, *The Roots of the Problem and the Person*, Anchor Bible Reference Library (New York: Doubleday, 1991), 398–99.

but Christ instituting the new Passover and giving himself as the true Lamb. This would be in harmony with 1 Corinthians 5:7 ("Christ, our Passover Lamb, has been sacrificed"), and it is also implied in John 19:36, where the sacrificial rubric of Exodus 12:46 (also Num 9:12) is applied to the crucified Jesus: "Not a bone of him shall be broken." Christ himself is the sacrificed Lamb, and the new Passover is his death and Resurrection, which fulfill the meaning of the old Passover. The content of this new Passover is signified in celebration of the Last Supper, when Jesus gives to his disciples bread and wine as his Body and his Blood.

The Words of Institution

The biblical Institution narratives fall into two distinct groups: Mark 14:22–25 is close to Matthew 26:26–29, both referring to the blood of the covenant of Mount Sinai (Ex 24:8), whereas Luke 22:14–20, which has an affinity to 1 Corinthians 11:23–27, highlights the new covenant of Jeremiah 31:31. While the fourth Gospel does not report the Institution of the Eucharist, it would appear that the momentous "bread of life" discourse of John 6 (especially verses 51–58) presupposes it. The dominical words of Institution fulfill all five "primary criteria" for sayings or deeds attributed to the historical Jesus, as developed in New Testament scholarship, especially the criterion of "multiple attestation"—not just of a general motif, such as "Kingdom of God", but of a precise saying and deed.[6]

[6] The five "primary criteria" listed by Meier are (1) embarrassment (the difficult idea of eating the flesh and drinking the blood of Christ); (2) discontinuity (the originality of Jesus' "new Passover"); (3) multiple attestation (as seen); (4) coherence (with the mission of Jesus and in particular with his Passion); and (5) Jesus' rejection and execution (the alienation caused by the difficulty and novelty of the words). Meier, *Marginal Jew*, 1:168–77.

While there is thus a strong plausibility that the dominical words at the Last Supper, as transmitted by Paul and the Synoptic Gospels, represent the *ipsissima vox* of Jesus (the "kind of thing" he would have said), the variations in the four accounts pose the question of the *ipsissima verba* (what exactly he said). Allowance needs to be made for the development of oral tradition and the work of a final redactor. There would seem to be a wide consensus among biblical scholars that Jesus indeed broke bread, gave it to his disciples, and said, "This is my body", thus anticipating the violent death he was about to suffer. Neither the Hebrew nor the Aramaic language use the copula "is", but it can be safely assumed that Jesus identified the broken and shared bread with his body and hence with the voluntary offering of his life.

The words over the chalice are usually considered to have undergone some post-Easter editing from different theological perspectives. The pre-Pauline and Lukan version, evoking a "new covenant", avoids the scandal to Jewish ears of drinking blood. However, the reference to Jeremiah 31:31 raises the difficulty that this passage has no explicit connection with sacrifice or the offering of blood, and it may represent a later addition, at least as it stands in First Corinthians. In Luke, the statement that the blood is shed "for you" (22:20) would suggest an already existing liturgical use. In favor of the version in Matthew and Mark, it can be argued that covenant, blood (sacrifice), and meal are already connected in Exodus 24:8, to which it alludes (see also Deut 12:7). Why should this stark version of the words of Institution as found in Matthew and Mark not be the authentic one, precisely because it is more difficult to understand and accept in a Jewish context? In an original way, the words of Jesus link the expectation of the Messiah with the suffering servant of Isaiah 53, who lays down his life "for many" (cf. 53:11, 12). To conclude, then, there is no compelling reason not to accept the origin of the words of Institution in Jesus himself. The Apostle Paul, who is usually regarded as the earliest witness to the Last Supper tradition (A.D. 53/54), claims to pass on what he has received from the Lord himself (1 Cor 11:23). The fact that he and Luke include the command "Do this in remembrance of me" (1 Cor 11:24; Lk 22:19) would imply a liturgical practice that was already observed in Christian communities.

2

The Quest for the Origins of the Eucharist

In a letter written to Pope Leo X in 1516, Erasmus of Rotterdam (d. 1536) buttressed the great project of Renaissance Humanism to return to the sources (*ad fontes*) with the claim that one could extract Christian doctrine "in a much purer and more vigorous way ... from the very sources".[1] In the history-conscious nineteenth century, Saint John Henry Newman (1801–1890) illustrated his theory of the development of doctrine (and worship) with a strikingly different image: "It is indeed sometimes said that the stream is clearest near the spring. Whatever use may fairly be made of this image, it does not apply to the history of a philosophy or belief, which on the contrary is more equable, and purer, and stronger, when its bed has become deep, and broad, and full."[2]

Written Sources and Oral Tradition

The search for the origins of Christian liturgy certainly vindicates Newman over Erasmus. The sources that have

[1] Desiderius Erasmus, *Opus Epistolarum Des. Erasmi Roterodami*, ed. Percy Stafford Allen, Helen Mary Allen, and Heathcote William Garrod, 12 vols. (Oxford: Clarendon Press, 1910), 2:185 (no. 384).

[2] John Henry Newman, *An Essay on the Development of Christian Doctrine*, 14th impression (London: Longmans, Green, 1909), 40.

come down to us are few and far between, and it is disputed to what extent they represent a normative Christianity. Moreover, as Joseph Ratzinger (Pope Benedict XVI) observed, "The Last Supper is the foundation of the dogmatic content of the Christian Eucharist, not of its liturgical form. The latter does not yet exist."[3] This liturgical form was shaped by apostolic tradition, which was initially handed down not by reference to written texts (books were luxury goods to which only few had access) but in fidelity to oral teaching, with a special role for memorization. The Apostle Paul offers an example of this process: he had already instructed the Christian community in Corinth about the Lord's Supper during his long stay in the city. In writing he addresses only the specific problems that arose and does not repeat his entire teaching. In fact, he prefers to resolve matters in person (1 Cor 11:34). Early Christian authors, such as Tertullian (d. after 220), Saint Cyprian of Carthage (d. 258), and Saint Basil of Caesarea (d. 379), confirm the importance of unwritten liturgical and devotional practice.[4]

The very nature of oral tradition frustrates the historian's effort at reconstruction; hence, our knowledge of liturgical practice in the earliest period is very limited and much scholarship in this field is hypothetical. The "breaking of the bread", which the Acts of the Apostles present as a "eucharistic celebration and proleptic participation in the messianic banquet",[5] is held "at home" (Acts 2:46;

[3] Joseph Ratzinger, "Form and Content of the Eucharistic Celebration", in *Theology of the Liturgy: The Sacramental Foundation of Christian Existence*, vol. 11 of *Joseph Ratzinger Collected Works*, ed. Michael J. Miller, trans. John Saward and Kenneth Baker, S.J. (San Francisco: Ignatius Press, 2014), 305.

[4] Tertullian, *On the Crown* 3–4; Cyprian of Carthage, *Letter* 62.1, 11; Basil of Caesarea, *On the Holy Spirit* 27.65–66.

[5] Scott Hahn, *Kinship by Covenant: A Canonical Approach to the Fulfillment of God's Saving Promises*, Anchor Yale Bible Reference Library (New Haven, CT, and London: Yale University Press, 2009), 234.

5:42). Hence, it is often concluded that the Eucharist was originally celebrated in a domestic setting, which could range from the town houses (*domus*) and country estates of the upper classes to apartments of different sizes. More recently, however, the idea of "house churches" has come under scrutiny, and scholars have argued for a more formal and hierarchical setting of early Christian liturgy.[6]

Malachi 1:11

A key text for the early Christian understanding of the Eucharist is Malachi 1:11: "From the rising of the sun to its setting my name is great among the nations, and in every place incense is offered to my name, and a pure offering." Against the background of blemished sacrifices offered by a corrupt priesthood, God announces, through his prophet, a "pure offering". The Hebrew word used here is *minhah*, which designates the bloodless meal offering, typically a baked loaf and wine libation, that accompanied the burnt offering in the Temple of Jerusalem (see Num 15:4–5). As early as in 1 Corinthians 10, this sacrifice to be offered "in every place" (not just in the Temple) was identified by Christians with the Eucharist.[7] In antiquity, the sacrifice of animals and of the produce of the land was at the very heart of religious worship, both pagan and Jewish (before the destruction of the Temple in A.D. 70). Through the words and actions of Christ at the Last Supper, the concept of sacrifice was not superseded but transformed. Hence, the Eucharist, while initially being linked with the community

[6] See Edward Adams, *The Earliest Christian Meeting Places: Almost Exclusively Houses?* (London: Bloomsbury, 2016), and Stefan Heid, *Altar und Kirche: Prinzipien christlicher Liturgie* (Regensburg: Schnell & Steiner, 2019), esp. 69–85.

[7] See also *Didache* 14; Justin Martyr, *Dialogue with Trypho* 41; Irenaeus of Lyon, *Against Heresies* IV.17–18; and many later references in the patristic tradition.

meal of the local church (as evident in *Didache* 9–10), was considered a sacrificial action (*Didache* 14) already in the early second century, if not before. Sharing in it required baptism and repentance. Even in the modest settings of the first two centuries, a sacred space (by necessity temporal, not permanent) was constituted through and in the ritual performed by the body of believers.

Saint Justin Martyr

The earliest description of a eucharistic celebration comes from mid-second-century Rome and is found in the *First Apology* of Saint Justin Martyr (d. c. 165), a defense of Christian faith and practice addressed to the emperor Antoninus Pius. Justin first gives an account of the post-baptismal Eucharist, and later he sketches a typical Sunday Eucharist. The *First Apology* is written for a presumed pagan readership, and therefore only the essential structure of the liturgy is given in language intelligible to those who are unacquainted with Christian faith and practice; no detailed information is provided about ritual elements or the contents of prayers. The basic elements of the Sunday Eucharist noted by Justin have remained the same over the centuries: scriptural readings ("memoirs of the apostles"—the Gospels—and "writings of the prophets"[8]), preaching, preparation of bread and wine mixed with water, prayers of praise and thanksgiving offered by "the one who presides" and concluded with a congregational "Amen", Communion shared among those present and

[8] Justin Martyr, *First Apology* 67, trans. Lawrence J. Johnson, vol. 1, *Worship in the Early Church: An Anthology of Historical Sources* (Collegeville, MN: Liturgical Press, 2009), 66–69 (nos. 243–46), with some modifications.

brought by deacons to those who are absent, and a final collection for those in need.[9] Notably, Justin emphasizes the unique character of the Eucharist by analogy with the Incarnation: just as Christ "assumed flesh and blood for our salvation", so too the bread and wine, "over which thanks have been given (*eucharistētheisan*) through a word of prayer that is from him", are "the flesh and blood of that incarnate Jesus who was made flesh."[10] The "word of prayer" I take to include the words of Institution, which Justin goes on to cite in the form familiar from Matthew (26:26, 28) and Mark (14:22, 24). The eucharistic offerings transformed into the Flesh and Blood of Christ—like Ignatius of Antioch writing around 110, Justin prefers the Johannine terminology of "flesh" (*sarx*—6:51–58) to "body" (*soma*)—nourish "our blood and flesh".[11] Access to the Eucharist is not indiscriminate but dependent on faith, baptism, and moral conduct.[12]

The Church Order Known as Apostolic Tradition

There is an ancient Church order (a collection of catechetical teachings and liturgical instructions that regulate the life of a particular community), the so-called *Apostolic Tradition*, which twentieth-century scholarship attributed to Hippolytus, a colorful figure in the Roman church. Hippolytus accused Pope Callistus (d. 222) of laxity in the absolution of sinners, so Hippolytus set himself up as the first antipope in history; however, he was eventually reconciled and died a martyr in 235. Hippolytus was believed to have compiled

[9] Ibid., 65 and 67.

[10] Ibid., 66.

[11] Ibid.

[12] See Ignatius of Antioch, *Smyrnaeans* 6,2 and *Romans* 7,3.

important information on liturgical practice in Rome, which possibly even predated his own time. However, recent studies have called this theory into question.[13] The extant document, originally written in Greek, without a title, comes from the Christian East and has no connection with Rome. It has no single author but is a compilation of liturgical texts that were in use in various geographical areas and subject to frequent modifications. Some of the material may go back even to the mid-second century, but most parts stem from later periods (up to the early fourth century). There is a Latin translation in a fifth-century manuscript from Verona, as well as versions in Oriental Christian languages. The text also influenced subsequent Church orders in the East (*Apostolic Constitutions* VIII; *Canons of Hippolytus*; *The Testament of Our Lord Jesus Christ*). None of these works preserve the whole text of the *Apostolic Tradition*, which includes ordination rites for bishops, priests, and deacons; regulations on various states of life in the Church; the rites of the catechumenate and of baptism; various prayers and blessings. The Rite of Ordination of a Bishop includes a highly developed model of a Eucharistic Prayer. In the renewed *Missale Romanum* (Roman Missal) of 1970, Eucharistic Prayer II follows this "Hippolytan" model (though with significant modifications). While the *Apostolic Tradition* does contain ancient material, it cannot be used as a source for Roman liturgy in the early third century. Its impact on the development of Western liturgy was minimal until the reforms after Vatican II.[14]

[13] See esp. Paul F. Bradshaw, Maxwell E. Johnson, and L. Edward Philips, *The Apostolic Tradition: A Commentary*, Hermeneia (Minneapolis: Fortress Press, 2002).

[14] The ancient text was also used for the revision of the Rite of Ordination of Bishops and for the restored Rite of Christian Initiation of Adults (RCIA).

3

The Third Century between Peaceful Growth and Persecution

The status of early Christians in the Roman Empire was precarious, and government officials often regarded them with suspicion, but actual persecution was local and sporadic before the middle of the third century. The brutal measures under the emperors Decius in 250 and Valerius in 258 affected Christian communities throughout the empire, but they were followed by a period of peaceful growth, until in 303 the emperor Diocletian unleashed the last Roman persecution of Christians before Constantine's official recognition of Christianity in 313.

Places of Worship

Dedicated church buildings appear in the second half of the third century. Eusebius of Caesarea speaks about the construction of large "churches"—he uses the specific Greek term *ekklesiai*—on the foundations of older buildings that had become too small for the growing congregations of Christians.[1] Eusebius also presents the destruction

[1] Eusebius of Caesarea, *History of the Church* VIII.1.5.

of churches as a characteristic of the Diocletianic persecution. These pre-Constantinian churches could be provided with precious objects for worship, as emerges from the report of a confiscation in the church of Cirta in North Africa dated May 19, 303.

The Temple background to early Christian worship calls into question the conventional narrative that the primitive Church identified herself exclusively as an eschatological body of believers, rejecting ideas of sacred space and seeing no need for places dedicated specifically to ritual and worship. In a recent study, Jenn Cianca argues that Christians met in sacred places that were by necessity temporal, not permanent, and were constituted through ritual, especially the Eucharist. Drawing on insights from social anthropology and ritual studies, Cianca proposes the conception of a ritually constructed sacrality, which "allows for an organic, slower-moving development of early Christian sacred space, rather than reading a sea change into the building of the Lateran in Rome".[2]

This new perspective also illumines the disputed question whether pre-Constantinian Christian references to "altar" should be interpreted metaphorically or whether they designate material objects actually used in worship. Phenomenologically, the wooden tables for the early Christian Eucharist were very different from the stone altars associated with the slaughter of animals in pagan worship. However, as Stefan Heid shows, the sacrality of an altar did not depend on its form or material but on

[2] Jenn Cianca, *Sacred Ritual, Profane Space: The Roman House as Early Christian Meeting Place*, Studies in Christianity and Judaism 1 (Montreal and Kingston: McGill-Queen's University Press, 2018), 167. A similar argument is made by Ann Marie Yasin, *Saints and Church Spaces in the Late Antique Mediterranean: Architecture, Cult, and Community*, Greek Culture in the Roman World (Cambridge: Cambridge University Press, 2009), 44.

its function. In classical antiquity, various objects could serve as an altar for offerings to the gods, including metal tripods, stone pillars, wooden tables, and massive stone altars.[3] Moreover, the fact that an item was not fixed but mobile did not make it profane. Against this background, a portable wooden table that was brought into a Christian meeting place for the Eucharist could nonetheless be considered an altar and be charged with sacredness.[4]

Times of Worship

When we come to consider the day and time for the celebration of the Eucharist, the importance of the first day of the Jewish week is evident in early Christianity. This is the day of Christ's Resurrection from the dead (Mk 16:2; Jn 20:1, 19), and it is observed in a special way by the community (Acts 20:7–12; 1 Cor 16:2). The "Lord's day" (Rev 1:10) is most likely to be identified with the first day of the week, and on this day the Eucharist is held (*Didache* 14). The *Epistle of Barnabas* has commonly been dated to 130–135, but in recent scholarship, support has grown for an earlier date around 96–98. In this letter, which some churches accepted as part of the canonical Scriptures, Christians are instructed to celebrate not the Sabbath but the first day of the week, which is acclaimed as the "eighth day, which is the beginning of another world".[5] This

[3] Stefan Heid, *Altar und Kirche: Prinzipien christlicher Liturgie* (Regensburg: Schnell & Steiner, 2019), 54–67.

[4] Ibid., 149–57.

[5] *Epistle of Barnabas* 15, 8–9, ed. and trans. Michael W. Holmes after the earlier work of J. B. Lightfoot and J. R. Harmer, 3rd ed., *The Apostolic Fathers: Greek Texts and English Translations* (Grand Rapids, MI: Baker Academic, 2007), 428 and 429.

eighth day is marked by a new creation because it is the day of Jesus' Resurrection.[6] In the middle of the second century, Justin Martyr also explains the special significance of "the day of the sun" for the celebration of the Eucharist by reference to the beginning of God's creation and to Christ's resurrection.[7]

Given that the Jewish day is reckoned to begin with sunset, the weekly celebration of the Eucharist may initially have taken place on Saturday evening after the end of the Sabbath, as is increasingly argued by scholars. By the early third century, however, Tertullian records that the "sacrament of the Eucharist",[8] or the "sacrifice" at "the altar of God",[9] is celebrated in the morning—presumably on Sunday.[10] Tertullian clearly distinguishes the Eucharist from the convivial "God's banquet" held in the evening.[11] Tertullian also testifies to the requirement to fast before receiving the Eucharist, as does the *Apostolic Tradition*, and this points to a morning celebration.[12] In the middle of the third century, Cyprian of Carthage confirms that the Eucharist, which he calls *dominicum* (literally, "that which belongs to the Lord"), is separate from the evening meal and is held in the morning in celebration of the Lord's Resurrection.[13]

[6] Ibid.

[7] Justin Martyr, *First Apology* 67 trans. Lawrence J. Johnson, vol. 1, in *Worship in the Early Church: An Anthology of Historical Sources*, 67.8 (Collegeville, MN: Liturgical Press, 2009), 68 (no. 246).

[8] Tertullian, *On the Crown* 3, trans. Lawrence J. Johnson, vol. 1, in *Worship in the Early Church*, 142 (no. 495).

[9] Tertullian, *On Prayer* 19, trans. Lawrence J. Johnson, vol. 1, in *Worship in the Early Church*, 134 (no. 475).

[10] Tertullian, *On the Crown* 3.3, and *On Prayer* 19.1–3.

[11] Tertullian, *To My Wife* 2.8.8, trans. Lawrence J. Johnson, vol. 1, in *Worship in the Early Church*, 136 (no. 484); also *Apology* 39.16–17; *On the Shows* 13.4.

[12] Tertullian, *To My Wife* 2.5.3; *Apostolic Tradition* 36.

[13] Cyprian of Carthage, *Letter* 62.16.

Facing East

In most religious traditions, the position taken in prayer and the layout of holy places is determined by a "sacred direction". From the second century onward, it was a matter of course for Christians to pray facing east.[14] The *Didascalia apostolorum*, a fourth-century Syriac Church order based on a Greek original believed to date to the early third century, rules that the liturgical assembly, both clergy and laity, should stand and turn toward the east in prayer.[15] The psalm verse adduced to authenticate this rule, "Give glory to God, who rides upon the heaven of heavens toward the east" (Ps 67:34 in the Greek Septuagint translation), is understood as a prophecy of the Lord's Ascension. Christ ascended toward the east, the place of Paradise (Gen 2:8), from where his Second Coming is expected. A broad stream of liturgical sources from the fourth century onward confirms the practice of facing east. The lifting up of hearts that introduced the Eucharistic Prayer (see below) was accompanied by prayer gestures of the entire assembly: standing upright, raising one's arms, looking upward, and turning toward the east.[16]

The Eucharist as Sacrifice

The works of Christian authors from different regions in the late second and early third centuries—including Irenaeus

[14] See Uwe Michael Lang, *Turning Towards the Lord: Orientation in Liturgical Prayer*, 2nd ed. (San Francisco: Ignatius Press, 2009), 35–71.

[15] *Didascalia apostolorum* 12.

[16] See Robert F. Taft, "The Dialogue before the Anaphora in the Byzantine Eucharistic Liturgy, II: The *Sursum corda*", *Orientalia Christiana Periodica* 54 (1988), 74–75.

of Lyon (d. 202), who was born in Asia Minor, Clement (d. c. 215) and Origen of Alexandria (d. 253), Tertullian (d. after 220) and Cyprian of Carthage (d. 258)—offer rich contributions to a theology of the Eucharist. Their varied lines of thought converge in a clear understanding of the sacrificial character of the Eucharist and a realistic sense of the presence of Christ in the consecrated offerings and of the salvific effects they bestow on those who receive them in faith. They also testify to the great reverence in which Christians held the Body and Blood of Christ. Of particular interest is Cyprian's very influential *Letter 63*, wherein he contends with groups who use water in place of wine for the Eucharist—a practice that is known from the Syrian *Acts of Thomas* and other New Testament apocrypha. Cyprian elaborates a theology of the Eucharist as the offering of an unbloody sacrifice in remembrance of the Passion of Christ. In the sacrifice of the Church, Christ, the High Priest of the New Covenant, offers himself, and the ordained priest acts in the Person of Christ by imitating what he did at the Last Supper.[17] Cyprian comments on the sacrificial connotation of wine in Old Testament prophecies and argues that its use is inseparable from the liturgical memorial of Christ's Passion. Moreover, to reject its consumption in the Eucharist is unfaithful to the Last Supper tradition. To underscore his argument, Cyprian cites the words of Institution from Matthew 26 and 1 Corinthians 11.[18]

[17] Cyprian of Carthage, *Letter* 63.14, 17.
[18] Ibid., 62.9–10.

4

Early Eucharistic Prayers: Oral Improvisation and Sacred Language

At the heart of the Eucharist stands the great prayer of thanksgiving, in which the offerings of bread and wine are consecrated as the Body and Blood of Christ. In the first two or three centuries, there was no fixed written form of liturgical prayer and room was given to improvisation, within a framework of stable elements and conventions that governed not only content but also structure and style in a manner that was largely indebted to biblical language. Allan Bouley notes that such "are ascertainable in the second century and indicate that extempore prayer was not left merely to the whim of the minister. In the third century, and possibly even before, some anaphoral texts already existed in writing."[1] Hence, Bouley identifies an "atmosphere of controlled freedom",[2] since concerns for orthodoxy limited the bishop's or priest's liberty to vary the texts of the prayer. This need became particularly pressing during the doctrinal struggles of the fourth century, and from then onward, the texts of Eucharistic

[1] Allan Bouley, *From Freedom to Formula: The Evolution of the Eucharistic Prayer from Oral Improvisation to Written Texts*, Studies in Christian Antiquity 21 (Washington, DC: The Catholic University of America Press, 1981), xv.

[2] Ibid.

Prayers, such as the Roman Canon and the Anaphora of Saint John Chrysostom, were codified.

Oral Transmission and Memorization

In a study on improvisation in liturgical prayer, Achim Budde analyzes three Oriental anaphoras used over a considerable geographical area: the Egyptian version of the Anaphora of Saint Basil, the West Syrian Anaphora of Saint James, and the East Syrian Anaphora of Nestorius.[3] Applying a comparative method, Budde identifies common patterns and stable elements of structure and style rhetoric, which he argues go back to the preliterary history of these Eucharistic Prayers and may have been transmitted by memorization. Budde's methodological approach is an important supplement and corrective to that of Bouley's, who would appear to underestimate the significance of memory in an oral culture. Sigmund Mowinckel, known especially for his exegetical work on the Psalms, has observed that rapid development of fixed forms of prayer corresponds to an essential religious need and constitutes a fundamental law of religion.[4] The formation of stable liturgical texts can thus be ascertained from early on as a strong force in the process of handing on the Christian faith.

The largely oral practice of early liturgical prayer means that only a few written anaphoras may be dated with some probability to the pre-Nicene period. Three texts are usually mentioned: the aforementioned model Eucharistic

[3] Achim Budde, "Improvisation im Eucharistiegebet: Zur Technik freien Betens in der Alten Kirche", *Jahrbuch für Antike und Christentum* 44 (2001): 127–44.

[4] Sigmund Mowinckel, *Religion und Kultus*, trans. Albrecht Schauer (Göttingen: Vandenhoeck & Ruprecht, 1953), 8, 14, 53.

Prayer from the *Apostolic Tradition*, the Anaphora of Addai and Mari, and the Strasbourg papyrus. However, questions regarding their date and possible early form elude definitive answers. Thus, the warning of the Anglican liturgist Kenneth Stevenson is worth quoting in full:

> Every liturgical expert on antiquity knows that Hippolytus might, conceivably, have been a sham Syrian archaizer, doing his own thing, out of favor with the Pope; Addai and Mari could have been mutilated beyond recognition at the time of Patriarch Iso'yahb's liturgical adjustments in the seventh century (which involved abbreviations) and the *Strasbourg* papyrus could be a fragment of an early anaphora that went on to include material now lost but quite different in style and content from the later (complete) Greek Mark. With compilers of liturgical texts, all things are possible.[5]

The Barcelona Anaphora

Of significant import is the research of Michael Zheltov on the so-called Barcelona Anaphora, which is found on the fourth-century papyrus P. Monts. Roca inv. 128–78. This Greek text of Egyptian origin is the oldest material witness to a highly developed Eucharistic Prayer.[6] The anaphora contains an opening dialogue; a prayer of praise and thanksgiving leading to the Sanctus; an oblation of the bread and the chalice; a first epiclesis asking the Father to send the Holy Spirit on the bread and chalice to make them the Body and Blood of Christ; an Institution narrative followed by an anamnesis; a second

[5] Kenneth Stevenson, *Eucharist and Offering* (New York: Pueblo, 1986), 9.

[6] Michael Zheltov, "The Anaphora and the Thanksgiving Prayer from the Barcelona Papyrus: An Underestimated Testimony to the Anaphoral History in the Fourth Century", *Vigiliae Christianae* 62 (2008): 467–504.

epiclesis asking for the spiritual fruits of Communion; and a concluding doxology.

Like the slightly later Strasbourg papyrus, the Barcelona Anaphora belongs to the Alexandrian tradition. The advanced form of this Eucharistic Prayer strongly supports the argument that the more recent Strasbourg papyrus is fragmentary and does not contain a full anaphora (as has been proposed). At the same time, the Barcelona text lacks some elements of the later Alexandrian tradition, such as the long intercessions that precede the Sanctus. Michael Zheltov also notes that the liturgical texts on the papyrus display archaic theological features (e.g., addressing Jesus as "child" or "servant" as in the *Didache* and the *Apostolic Tradition*), which might point to a third-century origin of the anaphora. The Barcelona Anaphora certainly calls for a revision of recent scholarship on the early development of Eucharistic Prayers. At the very least, it questions the theory advanced by Paul Bradshaw and Maxwell Johnson, among others, that elements, such as the Institution narrative and the epiclesis, should be considered a fourth-century interpolation. As Zheltov observes, "These parts do not have an interpolated but an organic nature."[7] If the Barcelona Anaphora can indeed be dated to the third century, it would increase the plausibility for a similar timeline for the Eucharistic Prayer in the *Apostolic Tradition*.

Liturgy and Sacred Language

Liturgical language is distinguished from other forms of Christian discourse by employing linguistic registers that express the community of faith's relation to the transcendent

[7] Ibid., 503.

in forms of praise, thanksgiving, supplication, intercession, and sacramental participation. The use of language in liturgy shows general characteristics that, to a varying degree, set it apart from everyday parlance. According to Christine Mohrmann, the early practice of improvisation within a stable framework led to a distinctly traditional style of liturgical prayer.[8] There exists a similar phenomenon in the field of literature, the stylized language of the Homeric epos with its consciously archaic and colorful word forms (*Homerische Kunstsprache*). The freedom of individual singers to improvise on the given material in epic poems helped to create a stylized language. The language of the *Iliad* and the *Odyssey*, which is also found in Hesiod and in later poetic inscriptions, was never a spoken language used in everyday life.[9]

With Mohrmann, we can name three characteristics of sacred or, as she also says, "hieratic" language. First, it tends to show tenacity in holding on to archaic diction (an example in contemporary English use would be "Our Father, who art in heaven ..."); second, foreign elements are introduced in order to associate with venerable religious tradition—for instance, the Hebrew biblical vocabulary in the Greek and Latin use of Christians, such as "amen", "alleluia", and *osanna* (this is already noted by Saint Augustine);[10] and third, liturgical language employs rhetorical figures that are typical of oral style, such as parallelism and antithesis, rhythmic clausulae, rhyme, and alliteration.

[8] Christine Mohrmann, *Liturgical Latin: Its Origins and Character, Three Lectures* (London: Burns & Oates, 1959), 24. Her collected studies are published in *Études sur le latin des chrétiens*, 4 vols. (Rome: Edizioni di Storia e Letteratura, 1961–1977).

[9] Mohrmann, *Liturgical Latin*, 10–11.

[10] Augustine of Hippo, *De doctrina Christiana* II.11.16.

5

After the Peace of the Church: Liturgy in a Christian Empire

In 313, the emperor Constantine granted Christianity toleration and legal status in the Roman Empire. This act was hailed as the "Peace of the Church". The Constantinian settlement provided social and material conditions in which the religious practice of ordinary Christians could flourish, and many new converts (though not all with pure motives) flocked into the newly built churches. From this period, the first written sources of liturgical texts emerge, and they usually carry the approbation of a bishop or a synod of bishops. It was widely considered necessary to formalize Christian worship in order to retain standards of doctrinal content and of prayer language. While the fourth century reshaped the celebration of the Eucharist, the theological and spiritual contents of these Eucharistic Prayers build on the foundations that were laid in the previous centuries.

The Antiochene Tradition

The leading episcopal sees of Antioch in Syria and Alexandria in Egypt are associated with the formation of the "classical" anaphoras of the Eastern Christian traditions. An early example of an Antiochene anaphora is found in the eighth book of the *Apostolic Constitutions*, a comprehensive Church order ascribed to Saint Clement of Rome but compiled in the region of Antioch between 375 and 400. *Apostolic Constitutions* VIII contains a complete eucharistic rite, which used to be known as the Clementine Liturgy. This account follows the pattern recorded by Justin in the mid-second century, but offers much more detail, listing four Scripture readings (law, prophets, epistle, Gospel); a sermon; the dismissal of catechumens, penitents, and other groups; prayers of the faithful in the form of a litany; the exchange of peace; offertory; anaphora; Communion rites; thanksgiving for Communion; and dismissal. The typical structure of the Antiochene Anaphora can be summarized as follows:[1]

Introductory dialogue with an initial Trinitarian greeting modeled on 2 Corinthians 13:14 ("The grace of ...")
Praise and thanksgiving ("It is truly right and just ...")
Introduction to the Sanctus
Sanctus
Post-Sanctus
Institution narrative
Anamnesis
Epiclesis
Intercessions
Doxology

The Byzantine Rite developed from the Antiochene liturgical family.[2] Within this tradition, the Eucharistic Prayer

[1] For a selection of ancient anaphoras in English translation with useful introductions, see R. C. D. Jasper and G. J. Cuming, *Prayers of the Eucharist: Early and Reformed*, 3rd ed. (Collegeville, MN: Liturgical Press, 1987).

[2] For a concise introduction with ample reference to further literature, see Robert F. Taft, *The Byzantine Rite: A Short History*, American Essays in Liturgy (Collegeville, MN: Liturgical Press, 1992).

with the greatest historical impact is the Anaphora of Saint John Chrysostom, which by the eleventh century had replaced the Byzantine version of the Anaphora of Saint Basil as the most frequently used in the Divine Liturgy (Eucharist). Robert Taft has made a compelling case that John Chrysostom, when he became bishop of Constantinople, introduced from his native Antioch an early form of the anaphora that bears his name, revising it for use in the capital.

Another important influence on the Byzantine Rite was the liturgical practice of Jerusalem, where stational liturgies at the holy sites proved to be very popular. This practice was imitated by pilgrims in their local churches, above all Constantinople and Rome.[3] The Jerusalem cycle of feasts had significant influence in both East and West. The Syriac liturgical traditions belong to the Antiochene family but also show particular and complex developments.[4]

The Alexandrian Tradition

The liturgical tradition of Alexandria, the center of Christianity in Egypt, is well documented and may reach back to the third century (see the section in chapter 4 on the Barcelona Anaphora). The typical elements of the Alexandrian Anaphora can be listed as follows:

Introductory dialogue ("The Lord be with [you] all ...")
Praise and thanksgiving ("It is truly right and just ...")
Intercessions (including the deceased)

[3] See John F. Baldovin, *The Urban Character of Christian Worship: The Origins, Development, and Meaning of Stational Liturgy*, Orientalia Cristiana Analecta 228 (Rome: Pont. Institutum Studiorum Orientalium, 1987).

[4] See the overview of Bryan D. Spinks, *Do This in Remembrance of Me: The Eucharist from the Early Church to the Present Day*, SCM Studies in Worship and Liturgy (London: SCM Press, 2013), 141–70.

Introduction to the Sanctus
Sanctus
Epiclesis I
Institution narrative
Anamnesis
Epiclesis II
Doxology

The two epicleses are a characteristic feature of the Alexandrian tradition. Regarding the first epiclesis, there seem to be two strands: On the one hand, sources such as the Barcelona Anaphora and the fragmentary Deir Balyzeh papyrus from Upper Egypt (between the sixth and eighth centuries) include a first epiclesis asking the Father to send the Holy Spirit upon the offerings of bread and wine to make them the Body and Blood of Christ. The second epiclesis, after the Institution narrative, petitions for the spiritual fruits of sacramental Communion. On the other hand, in the Eucharistic Prayer of Sarapion, in the fully developed Greek Anaphora of Saint Mark, and in its Coptic version, the Anaphora of Saint Cyril of Alexandria, the first epiclesis is less specific, asking for the blessing of the sacrifice through the coming of the Holy Spirit. Instead, the prayer for the Consecration of the eucharistic offerings forms part of the second epiclesis. Perhaps this could be seen as an assimilation to the Antiochene pattern. The Egyptian version of the Anaphora of Saint Basil, which is related but distinct from the Byzantine Basil and can be classified as West Syrian in structure, might have been used in Egypt since the mid-fourth century. The anaphora is known in its original Greek as well as in the Coptic dialects of Sahidic and Bohairic, and it became the standard anaphora of the Coptic Divine Liturgy.[5]

[5] On Egyptian anaphoras and the Coptic liturgy, see Spinks, *Do This in Remembrance of Me*, 94–120.

Scripture Readings

While there are no lectionary sources for the celebration of the Eucharist before the late fourth century, it is very likely that for major feasts and special seasons of the developing liturgical year, the appropriate pericopes—that is, "particular scriptural passages separated from their biblical context"[6]—were used from very early on. The selection of particular biblical texts can be expected above all for the annual celebration of Easter and structured the pre-paschal period of preparation that was to become the forty days of Lent, as well as the fifty days of the paschal season known since the late second century as Pentecost. The annual festivals of martyrs, such as Peter and Paul in Rome or Polycarp in Smyrna, would also have been associated with particular readings. Fixed readings for liturgical feasts and seasons are indicated in sermons and writings of Ambrose of Milan and Augustine of Hippo.

There is no evidence for the once popular theory that before the systematic organization of pericopes in the fourth and fifth centuries, there was a continuous or consecutive reading (*lectio continua*) of Scripture at the Eucharist. When early Christian theologians comment on an entire biblical book in the form of consecutive homilies, such as Origen in the first half of the third century and John Chrysostom in the late fourth century, this did not happen in the context of the Eucharist—leaving aside the question whether they delivered these homilies at all or whether they were literary products. At the celebration of the Eucharist, the presiding bishop would usually choose

[6] Cyrille Vogel, *Medieval Liturgy: An Introduction to the Sources*, rev. and trans. William G. Storey and Niels Krogh Rasmussen (Washington, DC: Pastoral Press, 1981), 300.

the readings, and there is no suggestion that he was bound to a continuous reading of a biblical book.

Liturgy and Music

It is often assumed that the chanting of psalms and the singing of hymns had a natural place in early Christian worship. However, Joseph Dyer cautions that "psalmody was not an essential component of the Mass from the beginning, and the *loci* appropriate for singing were only gradually occupied."[7] In Greco-Roman culture, singing at evening banquets was common, and Christians followed this custom, but this did not happen at celebrations of the Eucharist in the early morning.[8] Dyer also notes "the possibly thin line that separated stylised reading from simple song in the ancient world".[9] Thus, the formal recitation of texts could have provided an opening for the introduction of chanting psalms. By the late fourth century, psalms were sung in the eucharistic liturgy between the readings and during Communion (especially Psalm 34:8, which was an obvious choice because of the verse: "Taste and see that the LORD is good").

[7] Joseph Dyer, "Review of James McKinnon, *The Advent Project: The Later Seventh-Century Creation of the Roman Mass Proper*", *Early Music History* 20 (2001): 283.

[8] See Christopher Page, *The Christian West and Its Singers: The First Thousand Years* (New Haven, CT, and London: Yale University Press, 2010), 55–71, and his collection of sources at 72–83.

[9] Dyer, "Review", 284–85.

6

The Formative Period of Latin Liturgy

In the fourth century, the city of Rome was no longer the center of political power, but its classical culture maintained a grip on the elites of the empire. Beginning with Pope Damasus (r. 366–384), a conscious effort was made to evangelize the symbols of Roman culture for the Christian faith. Part of this project was the Christianization of public space through an extensive building program that was to transform Rome into a city dominated by churches.[1] Another important part of this project was the Christianization of public time; a cycle of Christian feasts throughout the year replaced pagan celebrations, as evident in the *depositio martyrum* of the Chronography of 354. This liturgical calendar, which can be dated to the year 336, begins with the Nativity of Christ (December 25) and lists the celebrations of martyrs in Rome together with the place in the city where they were commemorated.[2]

[1] See the beautifully illustrated volume by Hugo Brandenburg, *Ancient Churches of Rome from the Fourth to the Seventh Century: The Dawn of Christian Architecture in the West*, trans. Andreas Kropp, Bibliothèque de l'Antiquité Tardive 8 (Turnhout: Brepols, 2005).

[2] See Paul F. Bradshaw and Maxwell E. Johnson, *The Origins of Feasts, Fasts and Seasons in Early Christianity* (Collegeville, MN: Liturgical Press, 2011), 175.

Greek had a considerable place in the worship of the first Christian communities in Rome, and there are still traces of its use in the middle of the fourth century. The formation of a Latin liturgical idiom was also part of the wide-ranging effort to evangelize culture and cannot simply be described as the adoption of the vernacular language in the liturgy, if "vernacular" is taken to mean "colloquial". The Latin of the Canon, of the collects, and Prefaces of the Mass was a highly stylized form of speech, shaped to express complex theological ideas, and would not have been easy to follow by the average Roman Christian of late antiquity. Moreover, the adoption of *Latinitas* made the liturgy more accessible to most people on the Italian peninsula, but not to those in Western Europe or in North Africa whose native language was Gothic, Celtic, Iberic, or Punic.

The Canon of the Mass

The most important source for the early Roman Eucharistic Prayer is Ambrose of Milan's series of catecheses for the newly baptized, dating from around 390, known by the title *De sacramentis* (*On the Sacraments*). Ambrose notes that he follows the "pattern and form" of the Roman Church in everything; this would imply that the same Eucharistic Prayer from which he quotes was also used in Rome.[3] The prayers he cites correspond to the core of the later *Canon Missae*: the first epicletic prayer asking for the Consecration of the eucharistic offerings (*Quam oblationem*), the Institution narrative (*Qui pridie*), the anamnesis and act of offering (*Unde et memores*), the prayer for the

[3] Ambrose, *On the Sacraments* III.1.5.

acceptance of the sacrifice (*Supra quae*), and the second epicletic prayer for spiritual fruits of sacramental Communion (*Supplices te rogamus*).[4]

The earliest available physical witness to the Canon, albeit in a somewhat garbled form, is the *Bobbio Missal*, an important source for the Gallican tradition dating from the turn of the eighth century. The text that appears, with minor variations, in the mid-eighth-century Old Gelasian Sacramentary reflects Roman liturgical practice of the mid-seventh century, if not earlier. The differences between Ambrose's Eucharistic Prayer and the received Canon are far less remarkable than their similarities, given that the more than two centuries in between were a period of intense and dynamic liturgical development.

Rhetoric of Salvation

Liturgical prayer is a form of public speech, and hence in Christian antiquity, the threefold *officia* (duties or tasks) of classical rhetoric were applied to it as well: liturgical prayer is a means of teaching the faith (*docere*), the beauty of its language appeals to the worshippers' aesthetic sense (*delectare*), and its rhetorical force spurs the faithful on to a virtuous life (*movere*).[5] Hence, the liturgical prayers that have come down to us in the early medieval Roman sacramentaries were formed according to technical rules of composition. The rhetorical character of these texts is evident from the

[4] Ibid., IV.5.21–22; 6.26–27. The term "canon" seems to have been used first in the sixth century; the oldest known reference to "prex canonica" is Pope Vigilius, *Letter to Profuturus of Braga*, 5.

[5] See Mary Gonzaga Haessly, *Rhetoric in the Sunday Collects of the Roman Missal: With Introduction, Text, Commentary and Translation* (Cleveland: Ursuline College for Women, 1938), 5.

Eucharistic Prayer cited by Ambrose. For instance, the formula of petition "et petimus et precamur" ("we both ask and pray") is an example of a doubling of the verb, which is typical of classical (pagan) worship. This stylistic feature is also found in the *Te igitur* section of the Gregorian Canon, though without the alliteration: "supplices rogamus ac petimus" ("we make humble prayer and petition").

Another example for effective rhetoric in liturgical prayer is the accumulation of near synonyms. In Ambrose, the petition to accept the oblation is intensified by three epithets: "Make this offering for us approved, reasonable, acceptable (*scriptam, rationabilem, acceptabilem*)." In the prayer *Quam oblationem* of the Gregorian Canon, this sequence is increased to five epithets: "Which oblation be pleased, O God, we pray, to make in all things blessed, approved, ratified, reasonable, and acceptable (*benedictam, adscriptam, ratam, rationabilem, acceptabilemque*)", with the notable addition of the legal term "ratus" ("ratified, valid").

The Collects

The presidential prayers known as collects are later in origin than the Eucharistic Prayer and may go back to the first half of the fifth century. Their typical style is well established already in the earliest examples that have come down to us in the Verona manuscript (also known as the Leonine Sacramentary), which is from the first quarter of the seventh century but contains material that has been dated from 400 to 560. The style of the collects is terse, well-balanced, and economical in expression; each prayer consists generally of a single sentence, even if the syntax can at times be complex. In her study of the Sunday collects of the *Missale Romanum*, where the oldest euchological material of the

Roman Rite is preserved, Mary Gonzaga Haessly distinguishes between a protasis (prelude), which is "the basis or background for the Petition", and an apodosis (theme), which "is, in general, the part of the Collect that expresses the purpose of the Prayer, or the goal toward which it gravitates".[6] The protasis usually in some way anticipates the petition, which is in turn fulfilled in the apodosis. This structure can be illustrated with the example of a Sunday collect already contained in the Old Gelasian Sacramentary (mid-eighth century). The prayer is remarkable for its literary beauty and theological richness:

Almighty, ever-living God,
who in the abundance of your kindness surpass the merits
and the desires of those who entreat you,
pour out your mercy upon us:
to pardon what conscience dreads
and to give what prayer does not dare to ask.
Through our Lord . . .[7]

The Prefaces

It is a characteristic of Western liturgies that the Preface, originally considered the beginning of the Eucharistic Prayer, varies according to the liturgical season or feast. Its general theme, which is praise and thanksgiving for the divine economy of salvation, leads into the heart of

[6] Ibid., 13.

[7] Translation from *Roman Missal: Renewed by Decree of the Most Holy Second Ecumenical Council of the Vatican, Promulgated by Authority of Pope Paul VI and Revised at the Direction of Pope John Paul II*, English translation according to the third typical edition (London: Catholic Truth Society, 2011), Twenty-Seventh Sunday in Ordinary Time.

the eucharistic sacrifice. The Preface corresponds with the celebrant's call to the people, "Lift up your hearts (*Sursum corda*)", and shows a distinct lyrical tone. The great number of Prefaces in ancient Roman sources suggests that improvisation and new composition prevailed here for a longer duration than for other parts of the Mass. The exemplar of the Gregorian Sacramentary, sent by Pope Hadrian I to Charlemagne in the late eighth century (*Hadrianum*), has only fourteen Prefaces, and this pattern prevailed in the course of the Middle Ages, when the number of Prefaces became strictly limited. This pruning was arguably too drastic, but there were good reasons for it: many ancient Prefaces are profuse in style and content, and they introduce idiosyncratic themes that can detract from the praise and thanksgiving to God, which marks the opening of the Eucharistic Prayer. The *Missale Romanum* of 1570 has eleven Prefaces, to which several were added in the twentieth century. After the Second Vatican Council, the corpus of Prefaces was greatly expanded to eighty-one in the *Missale Romanum* of 1970, and more were added in the second and third typical editions.[8]

The fourth and fifth centuries were a crucial stage in the development of Latin liturgy. The Canon and the variable prayers of the Mass draw on the style of pagan prayer, but their vocabulary and content are distinctively Christian, indeed biblical. Their diction eschews the exuberance of the Eastern Christian prayer style, which is also found in the Gallican tradition. Many of the early collects are considered literary masterpieces. Christine Mohrmann rightly speaks of the fortuitous combination of a renewal of language,

[8] See *The Prefaces of the Roman Missal: A Source Compendium with Concordance and Indices*, ed. Anthony Ward and Cuthbert Johnson (Rome: C.L.V.–Edizioni liturgiche, 1989).

inspired by the newness of Christian revelation, and a stylistic traditionalism that was deeply rooted in the Roman world. The formation of this liturgical idiom contributed significantly to the comprehensive effort of Church leaders in late antiquity to evangelize classical culture.

7

Papal Stational Liturgy

In the late ancient and early medieval periods, celebrations of the Roman Mass can be distinguished into two types: the first, a pontifical type, is represented by the stational liturgy of the pope (or his delegate), which was held on Sundays and feast days during the liturgical year, and especially during Lent. A particular church of the city (*statio*) was assigned for a given day, and the pope with his attendant clergy would move in solemn procession from his residence at the Lateran Palace to the stational church to celebrate Mass. This kind of processional liturgy was first created in Jerusalem around the holy sites and was adopted in Constantinople in the late fourth century. Roman stational liturgy evolved in the sixth and seventh centuries, and it became such an integral part of the rite that the *statio* was recorded in the Mass formulary for specific days in the temporal cycle of the *Missale Romanum* until the post–Vatican II liturgical reform.

The second type of celebration, the simpler form of the rite, would have been observed in the twenty-five titular churches within the city walls, which can be compared to parish churches. We know very little about this presbyteral liturgy because the major sources from this time are mostly concerned with pontifical rites. In fact, the Eucharist offered by a priest (presbyter) was understood as a reduced form of the bishop's liturgy. There is a similar pattern in the Byzantine Rite, where the original function of the two processional entrances is still intelligible in the hierarchical (i.e., pontifical) Divine Liturgy, but was obscured when the entrances were adapted to the reduced presbyteral form.[1] In its hierarchical form, the presiding bishop enters the sanctuary for the first time from his cathedra in the nave of the church at the Little Entrance. During the Great Entrance, the bishop remains in front of the altar to receive the offerings, which in the liturgy of the Great Church of Constantinople (Hagia Sophia) were prepared in a separate room, the *skeuophylakion*.

Ordo Romanus I

Detailed instructions for the pope's solemn stational liturgy in Easter week are contained in the document known as *Ordo Romanus I*. This is in fact the oldest available ritual description of the Roman Mass, and it can be dated between the pontificate of Sergius I (r. 687–701) and the year 750, when there is evidence for its use north of the Alps. The rich and complex ritual described in *Ordo Romanus I* requires proficiency on the part of the liturgical actors and considerable logistical effort. Hence, it is likely that a master of ceremonies produced a written record that served as an aide-mémoire to train the sacred ministers and to make the material preparations for the elaborate ceremonial.[2]

[1] See Hans-Joachim Schulz, "Liturgie, Tagzeiten und Kirchenjahr des byzantinischen Ritus", in *Handbuch der Ostkirchenkunde, Band II*, ed. Wilhelm Nyssen, Hans-Joachim Schulz, and Paul Wiertz (Düsseldorf: Patmos, 1989), 36–37; also Alexander Schmemann, *Eucharist: Sacrament of the Kingdom*, trans. Paul Kachur (Crestwood, NY: St Vladimir's Seminary Press, 1987), 15–16.

[2] See the critical edition by Michael Andrieu, *Les Ordines Romani du haut moyen âge*, 5 vols., Spicilegium Sacrum Lovaniense 11, 23, 24, 28, 29 (Louvain:

We can discern two distinct cultural forces at work in the papal stational Mass: on the one hand, the ceremonial of the imperial court and administration (Rome was still part of the Byzantine Empire at the time), and on the other hand, the sacred (or hieratic) simplicity of the Roman Eucharist. Imperial ceremonial is evident especially in the procession of the pope on horseback with his court from the Lateran Palace to the stational church, and in the intricate entrance rite, wherein ecclesiastical officials carried before the pope a thurible and seven candles, which were signs of honor reserved to the emperor and senior magistrates. Some of this ceremonial is attached to the proclamation of the Gospel: the evangelary is carried in solemn procession, with lights and incense, to the elevated ambo.

In an influential paper with the title "The Genius of the Roman Rite",[3] the English liturgist Edmund Bishop spoke of the "simplicity" of the Roman Mass with specific reference to the early forms of the *Ordo Romanus*.[4] Such a characterization may be surprising, even if one recalls that the comparison is not made with de-ritualized modern forms of worship, but with the historical Byzantine and non-Roman Western rites. However, Bishop rightly notes that when we come to the core of the rite—the Eucharist—the atmosphere seems remarkably different: "It may be said that with this [namely, the proclamation of the Gospel] the ceremonial parts of the old Roman mass are over, just as

---

Peeters, 1931–1961), 2:67–108. An English version is found in John F. Romano, *Liturgy and Society in Early Medieval Rome*, Church, Faith and Culture in the Medieval West (Farnham: Ashgate, 2014), 229–48. For an earlier translation, published before Andrieu's edition, see E. G. C. F. Atchley, *Ordo Romanus Primus* (London: Moring, 1905), 117–49.

[3] Edmund Bishop, "The Genius of the Roman Rite", in *Liturgica Historica: Papers on the Liturgy and Religious Life of the Western Church* (Oxford: Clarendon Press, 1918), 1–19.

[4] Ibid., 8–12.

the sacrifice is about to begin."[5] In particular, the Canon of the Mass is said by the pope at the altar, with few liturgical gestures: signs of the cross over the offerings are indicated in Gelasian and Gregorian sacramentaries, perhaps dating back to the middle of the seventh century; however, the elevation of the species and profound bows are added only later in the course of the Middle Ages. At the heart of the solemn papal liturgy, ritual simplicity prevails.

The Role of Chant in the Mass

Ordo Romanus I brings into relief the fundamental role of chant in the celebration of Mass. Music does not simply serve as an ornament or embellishment but has a proper liturgical function. The trained singers of the schola cantorum have a distinct ministry in the hierarchically ordered assembly: first, in the Proper chants they proclaim texts that are (with some exceptions) drawn from Sacred Scripture. This musical proclamation serves to accompany and elucidate the meaning of a specific ritual (introit, offertory, communion), and it offers a meditation on the Word of God (gradual, alleluia, or tract). Second, in the ordinary chants (Kyrie, Gloria, Sanctus-Benedictus, and Agnus Dei), the schola sings on behalf of the entire congregation and thus forms a link between the pontiff with his assistants in the sanctuary and the faithful in the body of the church.[6]

[5] Ibid., 10.

[6] See Franck Quoëx, "Ritual and Sacred Chant in the *Ordo Romanus* Primus (Seventh–Eighth Century)", *Antiphon* 22 (2018): 218–19. The Western chant repertory contains a number of simple melodies for the ordinary chants that could well have been sung by the people. The evidence for such simpler chants appears later than for more sophisticated pieces. This is not surprising, if one considers that most of the early extant chant manuscripts were

The repertory of liturgical chant sung in Rome (and the surrounding territories in central Italy) in the early medieval period is known as Old Roman chant. The codification of this plainchant "dialect" occurred considerably later than that of the Gregorian repertory, and the five complete manuscripts with musical notation that have come down to us date from the eleventh to the thirteenth centuries. These manuscripts were created in a period when Gregorian chant was gaining ground in the city of Rome and eventually replaced the Old Roman tradition in the pontificate of Innocent III (r. 1198–1216).

How to Read Liturgical Sources

Interpreting the extant sources of the papal stational liturgy present us with a fundamental problem, since they are prescriptive texts that communicate how the rite *should* be enacted. As historical scholarship has made us increasingly aware, we cannot simply assume that such prescriptions are identical with the way in which the liturgy was in fact carried out. *Ordo Romanus I* was originally designed for the solemn papal Mass in Easter week; as a template for other occasions, it was likely to be adapted to the spatial arrangements, local resources, and (quite possibly) particular observances of the stational church chosen for the day. Moreover, it is a script for liturgical actors who were, for the most part, clerics (the papal court included also lay officials). As such, *Ordo Romanus I* can easily give the impression of a "clericalized" liturgy, but such a view would be misleading since

composed for the use of the schola cantorum and for individual cantors. Chants to be sung by the assembly may have been transmitted orally, without the need for writing them down.

it abstracts from the genre and purpose of the document. Liturgical sources from this period are not concerned with how people in general participated in the rite, let alone how they experienced it. Thus, *Ordo Romanus I* leaves many questions that would interest us unanswered. Nonetheless, it is a historical document of the greatest significance and, with hindsight, proved to be foundational for the further development of Western liturgy.

8

Codification of Liturgical Books

The age of transition from late antiquity to the early Middle Ages saw a codification of liturgical books for the celebration of Mass and other sacramental rites. These books typically contained the texts needed for specific liturgical ministers, above all the sacramentary for the officiating bishop or priest, the lectionary (and its preceding forms) for deacon, subdeacon, or lector, and the gradual, or Mass antiphoner, for the singers.[1]

Sacramentaries

The sacramentary can be described as the book containing the texts recited or chanted by the bishop or priest officiating at the celebration of Mass and other sacraments, as well as various consecrations and blessings. In the case of the Mass, formularies for particular occasions seem to have originated as small booklets (*libelli missarum*), which were collected and then organized into a book to be used

[1] For a detailed account, see the indispensable work of Cyrille Vogel, *Medieval Liturgy: An Introduction to the Sources*, rev. and trans. William G. Storey and Niels Krogh Rasmussen (Washington, DC: Pastoral Press, 1981).

throughout the liturgical year. Two types of Roman sacramentary have been identified, the Gelasian and the Gregorian. These differ from each other in significant ways but were both in use at the same time, in Rome and the Italian peninsula, as well as north of the Alps.

The Gelasian-type sacramentary is believed to have been compiled originally for the use of priests in the city's titular churches. Its oldest representative, the manuscript Reg. lat. 316 from the Vatican Library, known as the Old Gelasian, is organized in three distinct parts and keeps the temporal and the sanctoral cycles separate. Moreover, Mass sets typically have two collects (*oratio*), a secret (*secreta*),[2] a proper Preface (also called *contestatio* or *contestata*), a post-Communion (*post communionem*), and usually a prayer of blessing (*ad populum*).

The Gregorian-type sacramentary emerged from the collection of Mass books for the use of the pope when he celebrated at the Lateran (his cathedral) and in the stational churches of the city. Its earliest redaction may have been under Pope Honorius I (r. 625–638), and it was expanded in the course of the seventh and eighth centuries. The temporal and sanctoral cycles are combined into one sequence of Sundays and feast days. The Mass sets in the Gregorian tradition typically have three orations: a collect (*oratio*), a prayer over the offerings (*super oblata*), and a concluding prayer (*ad completa* or *ad complendum*); many formularies also include a prayer of blessing (*super populum*). The number of Prefaces is much smaller than in the Gelasian sacramentaries: the *Hadrianum* only has fourteen, compared to fifty-four in the Old Gelasian.

[2] The prayer more likely derives its name from the fact that it was said over the offerings that were "set apart" for the eucharistic Consecration, rather than from its recitation at a low voice.

Lectionaries

Lectionaries containing the texts of the scriptural readings (also called pericopes) for the Mass and the Divine Office developed, first, from marginal notes in biblical manuscripts designating the pericopes to be read and, second, from lists indicating the beginning (*incipit*) and the ending (*explicit*) of the readings for a particular liturgical celebration. Such lists, to be used with a Bible manuscript, are known as *capitularia* and were compiled for the epistle readings (chosen from the New Testament letters, the Acts of the Apostles, or the Old Testament), or for the Gospel readings, or for both sets of Mass readings. As a subsequent step, the full text of the scriptural readings was copied in a manuscript, either for the epistle (epistolary) or for the Gospel (evangelary), or for all the readings in a single Mass lectionary (later also included in a plenary missal together with the orations and the chants).

Non-Roman Western rites, such as the Gallican, Milanese, or Visigothic, show considerable variety in the selection of biblical pericopes for the celebration of Mass; however, they have features in common that distinguish them from the Roman Rite, above all the use of three readings, the first from the Old Testament (usually a prophecy), the second from the New Testament, and the third from the Gospels. In the Roman and Byzantine rites, only two readings are ordinarily given, and in the Byzantine tradition, the non-Gospel reading was strictly limited to the New Testament. There is no clear evidence that the early Roman Mass ever had a system of three readings.[3]

[3] See Aimé-Georges Martimort, "À propos du nombre des lectures à la messe", *Revue des Sciences Religieuses* 58 (1984): 42–51, and *Les lectures liturgiques et leurs livres*, Typologie des sources du Moyen Âge occidental 64 (Turnhout: Brepols, 1992).

The surviving documents indicate a complex history that is connected with the progressive organization of the liturgical year.[4] The choice of scriptural pericope was sometimes related to the particular church in Rome where the stational Mass was celebrated.

Epistle and Gospel readings were organized in two distinct cycles and were recorded in two kinds of liturgical books, which remained independent for some time. There was certainly no systematic construction of the lectionary as happened in the liturgical reforms after the Second Vatican Council. At the same time, however, there was some correspondence between the epistolary and the evangelary in the different stages of their development.[5]

The oldest extant lectionary source in which epistle and Gospel readings are joined together for a complete cycle of Sundays and feast days is a document that was to assume a crucial role for the subsequent history of the Roman Mass: the late-eighth-century *Comes* of Murbach.[6] Originating from an abbey in Alsace that acquired considerable religious and political importance in the Carolingian age, the extant *capitulare* lists the initial and in many cases also the concluding words of the epistle and Gospel readings and is meant to be used in conjunction with a Bible manuscript containing the full text. The arrangement of readings has been identified as a Frankish adaptation of earlier Roman epistolary and evangelary types. This fully

[4] See the classic work of Thomas J. Talley, *The Origins of the Liturgical Year* (New York: Pueblo, 1986), and the excellent summary of Vogel, *Medieval Liturgy*, 304–14.

[5] See Antoine Chavasse, *Les lectionnaires romains de la messe au VIIe et au VIIe siècle: Sources et dérivés*, Spicilegii Friburgensis Subsidia 22, 2 vols. (Fribourg, Switzerland: Editions Universitaire, 1993).

[6] The text was edited by André Wilmart, "Le Comes de Murbach", *Revue Bénédictine* 30 (1913): 25–69.

developed cycle of Sundays and feast days was adopted in the missals according to the use of the Roman curia of the thirteenth century and is largely the same as in the *Missale Romanum* of 1570.

Chant Books

The earliest Western sources for chant texts in the Mass originate from fifth-century Gaul and are associated with scriptural readings. Roman chant books are mentioned in Anglo-Saxon sources from the mid-eighth century. However, the oldest available sources of chant texts for the Roman Mass stem only from the late eighth century and were written in northern Francia.[7] These manuscripts do not contain musical notation. David Hiley explains that chant melodies "had previously been performed, learned, and transmitted without the aid of any written record (and thus they continued, to a considerable extent)."[8]

The codification of chant melodies most likely resulted from the considerable expansion of their repertory in the Carolingian period. The increasing number of chants and the greater stylistic variety of liturgical music (including sequences, tropes, and more settings of the ordinary) stretched the capacities for oral transmission and necessitated written aids for memorization, at least for the purpose of rehearsal, if not performance. Books with a complete cycle of notated chants emerge around the year 900, and the earliest examples are the manuscripts

[7] The six oldest manuscripts were published by René-Jean Hesbert, *Antiphonale Missarum Sextuplex* (Paris and Brussels: Vromant, 1935; repr., Rome: Herder, 1967).

[8] David Hiley, *Western Plainchant: A Handbook* (Oxford: Clarendon Press, 1993), 362.

Chartres, Bibliothèque Municipale 47 (hailing from Brittany), Laon, Bibliothèque Municipale 239, and Saint Gall, Stiftsbibliothek 359.

Ordines

An invaluable source for our understanding of early medieval Western liturgy is the collection of documents known as *Ordines Romani*, which describe actual rites and serve as practical instructions for actors in a variety of liturgical celebrations, including Mass, Divine Office, baptism, and other sacraments, as well as sacramentals (to use the later, scholastic distinction). These ordines were copied, adapted, and modified while being in liturgical use. The earliest manuscripts from the Carolingian period do not originate from the city of Rome but were written in Frankish territory and document a process of reception and adaptation of the Roman liturgy. For the history of the liturgy's actual performance (as well as its social and cultural impact) ordines are more informative than sacramentaries, because they offer us ritual "stage directions".

By the early eighth century, the Roman Rite was established as a recognizable body of liturgical texts and ritual forms, which were codified in liturgical books. These books were not composed originally with the intention of being copied and used beyond the city and its environs. For a variety of religious, cultural, and political reasons, Roman liturgical practice was adopted in northern and western Europe, especially in the Carolingian reform.

9

The Frankish Adoption and Adaptation of the Roman Rite

The city of Rome, the hallowed place of the martyrdom of the Apostles Peter and Paul and the see of the successor of Peter, attracted many pilgrims who were deeply impressed by the liturgical celebrations they witnessed and were keen to see some of their elements introduced back in their homelands. An important landmark was Pope Gregory the Great's sending of Augustine and his monastic companions to England in the late sixth century. The highly successful evangelization of the Anglo-Saxons and its wider cultural impact were specifically linked with Roman observances, strengthened the position of the papacy, and prepared the ground for Anglo-Saxon missionaries and scholars to work on the continent in the following century.

The Rise of the Carolingian Dynasty

The eighth century saw the rise of the Carolingian family to the Frankish throne, and their strong alliance with the papacy was to shape the history of Europe.[1] Pippin

[1] A good overview of the period is offered by Joseph H. Lynch and Phillip C. Adamo, *The Medieval Church: A Brief History*, 2nd ed. (London and New York: Routledge, 2014), 72–84.

the Short, king of the Franks from 751 to 768, introduced Roman chant with the support of leading bishops in his realm. This was not just a matter of musical preference but had profound implications for the choice of liturgical texts and the structure of the liturgical year. Thanks to what James McKinnon called the "Frankish absorption and transformation of the Roman chant", the repertory we know as "Gregorian" was created.[2]

Pippin's son and successor, known as Charles the Great or Charlemagne (born 742 or 747/748, king 768, emperor 800, died 814), resumed the work of his father with great energy. Charlemagne understood himself as a Christian Caesar who would renew the Roman Empire in union with the papacy. He not only enlarged the Frankish Empire until it extended from central Italy to the North Sea and from the Spanish March to the Elbe River, but also promoted a program of reform aiming at "the Christianization of society through education".[3] Charlemagne's legislation is shot through with admonitions and appeals for a reform that is meant to promote "unanimity with the Apostolic See and the peaceful harmony of God's holy Church".[4] While this demand included the use of Roman liturgical books, diverse sacramentaries continued to be used, combining Roman-Gregorian, Roman-Gelasian, and Gallican material.

At the same time, the Carolinian reform gave the Mass a ritual structure and shape that would essentially be retained

[2] James McKinnon, *The Advent Project: The Later Seventh-Century Creation of the Roman Mass Proper* (Berkeley, Los Angeles, and London: University of California Press, 2000), 3.

[3] Susan Keefe, *Water and the Word: Baptism and the Education of the Clergy in the Carolingian Empire*, Publications in Medieval Studies, 2 vols. (Notre Dame, IN: University of Notre Dame Press, 2002), 1:2.

[4] Charlemagne, *Admonitio generalis* 80, Monumenta Germaniae Historica, Legum Sectio II, *Capitularia Regum Francorum*, *Tomus* I, 61.

for over a millennium. Frankish liturgists adapted *Ordo Romanus I* as the standard and measure of the celebration of Mass to the local conditions and customs of their cathedrals and churches. In doing so, they ensured that the solemn pontifical liturgy remained the normative exemplar, in which all other celebrations of the Eucharist participated to a greater or lesser degree.

Personal and Emotive Liturgical Expression

The Frankish adaptation of the Roman Rite has been described as a shift toward a more personal, emotive understanding of and approach to the liturgy. The Gallican tradition shows a strong sense of spiritual introspection and of personal involvement in ministering at the altar. This tendency can be identified in the incorporation of specific prayers of a distinct style or register into the already existing structure of the Roman Mass. Such prayers known as apologies (*apologiae*) are composed in the first person (singular or plural) and make the bishop or priest celebrant enter into a personal dialogue with God, in which he acknowledges his sinfulness and expresses his fervent hope of receiving divine mercy in the form of a worthily offered Mass.[5] These prayers tend in a more penitential direction, which corresponds with the increasing focus on the priest as acting in the Person of Christ in the re-presentation of the sacrifice of the Cross.

[5] Such "apologies" are also known in the Byzantine tradition, and the oldest known example from the Divine Liturgy is the prayer "No one is worthy" (Οὐδεὶς ἄξιος), which may go back to the late seventh century. See Alain-Pierre Yao, *Les "apologies" de l'Ordo Missae de la Liturgie Romaine: Sources—Histoire—Théologie*, Ecclesia orans. Studi e ricerche 3 (Naples: Editrice Domenicana Italiana, 2019), 37–42.

Silence and Liturgical Prayer

The earliest clear evidence for a partial recitation of the Eucharistic Prayer in a low voice is found in the East Syrian tradition, in Narsai's *Homily on the Mysteries* from the late fifth or early sixth century. The inaudible recitation of large parts of the anaphora by the celebrant also spread to Greek-speaking churches by the middle of the sixth century. Gallican and Mozarabic liturgies also witness to the practice of saying prayers quietly, while the cantors would sing. In the *Ordines Romani*, we can identify a development from the understanding of the Canon of the Mass as a "holy of holies", into which only the pontiff could enter, toward its recitation *submissa voce*. We also need to keep in mind that, before the age of electrical amplification, when the pope celebrated Mass in one of the larger Roman basilicas, such as the Lateran, or St. Peter's in the Vatican, it would have been impossible in most parts of the church to follow the prayers he recited or chanted at the altar. Even in a smaller church, the audibility of the liturgical prayers would be limited. Just as there were *visible* barriers, such as the relatively high *cancelli* separating various precincts of the church's interior, and a *ciborium* over the main altar, likewise the physical dimensions of the church interior created an *acoustic* separation between the pope and his assistants at the altar and the faithful in the nave.

Local Reform and Practical Reach

The physical settings of liturgical worship in central and western Europe were for the most part very simple. There was a considerable gap between the cathedrals of episcopal towns and the humble chapels associated with rural settlements, with the churches of religious communities somewhere in between. At the same time, even plain buildings could have a relatively ornate interior, especially around the altar. Churches in economically prosperous areas were certainly provided with liturgical objects made of precious materials.

Synodal decrees and ecclesiastical capitularies from the early Middle Ages insist that priests should know and understand the texts they recite, celebrate the Divine Office diligently, care for their churches, look after relics, make sure bells are rung to call the faithful to prayer, and so on. Likewise, synods and individual bishops exhort the faithful not to talk idly when they are in church but to be attentive and prayerful during liturgical services—and not leave before the Mass is concluded.[6] The elevated Latin of liturgical prayer raised obstacles for comprehension even among Romance-speakers. Lay literacy was very limited in the early Middle Ages, and collections of devotional prayers (*preces privatae*) were the privilege of a small elite. When it came to musical resources, there must have been great disparity between episcopal and monastic centers, and the rural churches that served the majority of the people. Complex chants melodies required trained singers, and only simple responses and refrains would allow for popular involvement. Still, Charlemagne's *Admonitio generalis* assumes that the people join in the acclamations at Mass and explicitly mentions the Sanctus.[7] At any rate, it would be anachronistic to evaluate liturgical life in the Carolingian period by modern criteria of active participation, which are largely based on speaking roles. The efforts to raise the dignity and splendor of divine

[6] See Andreas Amiet, "Die liturgische Gesetzgebung der deutschen Reichskirche in der Zeit der sächsischen Kaiser 922–1023", *Zeitschrift für schweizerische Kirchengeschichte* 70 (1976): 103, 269.

[7] *Admonitio generalis*, c. 70.

worship, along with the emphasis on a broad education in the essentials of the Christian faith, no doubt increased the lay faithful's ability to enter into the celebration of the sacred mysteries.

Reassessing the Carolingian Reform

The success of the Roman-Gregorian liturgy throughout Western Europe was not simply a result of its imposition by royal and ecclesiastical authority, but owing to its religious and cultural appeal, as well as its ability to integrate Gallican elements. It was not rare in liturgical scholarship of the mid-twentieth century to present this synthesis in disparaging terms and to call for a return to pure and pristine Roman tradition (a principle that was implemented in the reforms after Vatican II only in parts). We are now in a better position to appreciate the enrichment that the Carolingian reform brought to the Roman Mass, and I would suggest that, because of its (necessarily) slow and gradual pace, its dependence on local initiative, and its focus on education (first of the clergy and, through them, of the whole people), it is a reform that merits the disputed epithet "organic". At the beginning of the second millennium, this process came full circle, and the mixed Roman-Frankish Rite was established in the papal city itself.

10

Monastic Life and Imperial Patronage

In the late ninth century, the city of Rome entered into a period of crisis, which has with some justification been called a "dark age" (*saeculum obscurum*) of the papacy, lasting well into the eleventh century. Spiritual and cultural leadership was found north of the Alps, and this held for the liturgy, too, which flourished in episcopal cities and Benedictine monasteries on both sides of the Rhine, such as Tours, Corbie, Metz, Mainz, Lorsch, Fulda, Reichenau, and Saint Gall. New impulses came with the monastic reform movements, above all from Cluny, and with the German emperors of the Ottonian dynasty. Like their Carolingian predecessors, the Ottonians took a vivid interest in ecclesiastical matters and showed themselves patrons of the liturgy in their realm, which also led to a flourishing of sacred architecture and art.

The Ordo Missae

The most momentous step in early medieval liturgical development was the organization of the recurring parts of the eucharistic celebration into what is known to this day as the *Ordo Missae* (Order of Mass). The earliest vestiges of such an order are already found in many Gregorian-type sacramentaries, which begin with a separate section entitled "How the Roman Mass is to be celebrated (*Qualiter missa romana caelebratur*)". These instructions correspond to the description of the papal stational liturgy in *Ordo Romanus I* and may have originated in the late seventh century.

A subsequent step was taken with collections of private prayers to be said by the celebrant at different moments of the rite. The earliest known example of such a collection is attested in the Sacramentary of Amiens (Paris, Bibliothèque Nationale, lat. 9432), dating from the second half of the ninth century.[1] Most of these texts, some of which consist only of a single psalm verse, accompany and elucidate the spiritual meaning of particular ritual actions for the celebrant priest. They thus serve to sustain his personal piety and help the devout offering of the sacrifice of the Mass.

The *Ordo Missae* as a distinct liturgical genre flourished between the ninth and eleventh centuries.[2] Contents and form varied considerably: for prayers, the opening word or phrase or the complete text is given; more or less detailed ritual instructions are sometimes provided;[3] and occasionally musical notation is added. Some ordines could be excessive in their use of private priestly prayers, above all the ordo produced for Sigebert, bishop of Minden in northern Germany from 1022 to 1036. The text has achieved some notoriety since it was published in 1557 by the Lutheran theologian and historian Matthias Flacius Illyricus (1520–1575) and became known as *Missa Illyrica*. Other ordines,

[1] The digitized manuscript is accessible at https://gallica.bnf.fr/ark:/12148/btv1b9065879n.

[2] See the seminal study by Bonifaas Luyxk, "Der Ursprung der gleichbleibenden Teile der heiligen Messe (Ordinarium Missae)", *Liturgie und Mönchtum* 29 (1961): 72–119; for a concise overview, see Alain-Pierre Yao, *Les "apologies" de l'Ordo Missae de la Liturgie Romaine: Sources—Histoire—Théologie*, Ecclesia orans. Studi e ricerche 3 (Naples: Editrice Domenicana Italiana, 2019), 355–58.

[3] Because of the red ink commonly used for such instructions, they have become known as "rubrics" (from *ruber*, the Latin word for "red").

however, are more measured in tone and less likely to overlay the traditional sequence of the rite of Mass. This testifies to an effort of pruning that resonates with views of the chronicler and Gregorian reformer Bernold of Constance (c. 1050–1100), who objects to the length and the private character of such prayers.[4] The shift from an oral to a written culture in the high medieval period gave the codified liturgical text a renewed importance. The pruned form of the *Ordo Missae* became normative for the celebration of the Eucharist and was incorporated into the thirteenth-century missal of the Roman Curia.

Modern liturgical scholarship has tended to interpret the creation of the *Ordo Missae* as a departure from the "classical form" of the Roman Rite that was determined by the cultural needs of the Franco-Germanic people. Joanne Pierce and John F. Romano offer a balanced version of this critique:

> The Roman Mass before this point was known for its soberness, simplicity, and straightforwardness. These OMs filled out the framework of the Roman Rite with new prayers, psalms, and gestures, elaborating the "soft spots" of the liturgy that had not previously received full elaboration, especially actions that occur without words. They imbued the Roman Eucharistic liturgy with new embellishment, drama, and allegorical symbolism.[5]

This assessment is not without problems: first of all, the characterization of the Roman Mass as sober, simple, and straightforward. The ritual shape of the Mass, for which *Ordo Romanus I* is our key witness, certainly featured lavish

[4] Bernold of Constance, *Micrologus de ecclesiasticis observationibus* 18.

[5] Joanne M. Pierce and John F. Romano, "The *Ordo Missae* of the Roman Rite: Historical Background", in *A Commentary on the Order of Mass of the Roman Missal*, ed. Edward Foley et al. (Collegeville, MN: Liturgical Press, 2011), 21.

and dramatic elements, especially in its processional parts, which were indebted to imperial ceremonial. Second, the elaboration of the "soft spots" can be understood as offering genuine development and even enrichment. For instance, the pontiff's moment of silent prayer before he approached the altar[6] occasioned the recitation of Psalm 42[43]:4, with the evocative antiphon "Introibo ad altare Dei" ("I will go to the altar of God").[7]

Third, and perhaps most importantly, the *Ordo Missae*, rather than offering drama and embellishment, above all provided a coherent (and memorable) scheme that facilitated the success of the "private Mass", with its much-reduced ceremonial. The shift toward the personal devotion of the offering priest gives some credence to the oft-repeated charge that the early medieval period saw a "clericalization" of the Mass and a detachment of the laity from its liturgical enactment.

The Creed at Mass

The last Ottonian ruler, the devout Henry II (king 1002, emperor 1014, d. 1024), who took great interest in ecclesiastical matters, is known to liturgical historians above all for his initiative to insert the Creed into the Roman Mass. The creed in question was that of the first two ecumenical councils of Nicaea (325) and Constantinople (381), which had been used as a baptismal profession of faith in the Christian East since the fourth century. Timothy I, anti-Chalcedonian patriarch of Constantinople (r. 511–517),

[6] *Ordo Romanus I*, 50.

[7] This psalm verse was already employed by Ambrose of Milan in his mystagogical catecheses for the newly baptized to evoke the approach to the altar of the Eucharist. *On the Sacraments* 4.2.7; *On the Mysteries* 8.43.

is credited with the introduction of the Creed into the eucharistic liturgy. In the early sixth century, the Creed was recited in the Byzantine Divine Liturgy after the proclamation of the Gospel and the dismissal of catechumens. In the Latin West, the Creed became part of the Mass first in Visigothic Spain, after the conversion of King Reccared and his nobles to Catholic Christianity. At the third synod of Toledo in 589, it was decreed that the Niceno-Constantinopolitan Creed should be said by the people at every Mass, in preparation for Holy Communion, preceding the Lord's Prayer.[8] By the middle of the seventh century, the Creed was said in the Visigothic Rite with the *filioque* clause, affirming the procession of the Holy Spirit from the Father and the Son. The Stowe Missal (c. 792–803), an important source for Irish liturgical use, places the Creed after the Gospel. Toward the end of the eighth century, Charlemagne had the singing of the Creed (including the *filioque*) inserted after the Gospel at the celebration of Mass in his Palatine chapel at Aachen. This decision was part of the Carolingian struggle against Adoptionist Christology in Spain. Pope Leo III (r. 795–816) reluctantly approved of the use of the Creed at Mass, though without the *filioque*, and he did not adopt the practice in Rome itself. The new custom spread slowly throughout the Carolingian realms and was commonly accepted in Franco-German churches by the tenth century.[9]

[8] The Latin translation of the Creed used in Mozarabic sources is different from the version later introduced in the Roman Rite. Interestingly, the loan-word *homusion* is used, where the Roman version translates *consubstantialis*; see Marius Férotin, *Le Liber Mozarabicus Sacramentorum et les manuscrits mozarabes*, Monumenta Ecclesiae Liturgica 6 (Paris: Firmin-Didot, 1912), 773.

[9] See the excellent documentation of Andreas Amiet, "Die liturgische Gesetzgebung der deutschen Reichskirche in der Zeit der sächsischen Kaiser 922–1023", *Zeitschrift für schweizerische Kirchengeschichte* 70 (1976): 222–28.

Staying in the city of Rome in 1014 for his coronation as emperor, Henry was surprised to find that, unlike in Germany, the Creed did not form part of the rite of Mass and petitioned Pope Benedict VIII (r. 1012–1024) to add it. Subsequently, the Creed was adopted in Rome on Sundays and on major feasts that celebrate an article of faith mentioned in it or that are otherwise connected with it (for example, the apostles as proclaimers of the faith). Thus, the Credo became a festive chant for particular days of the liturgical year, unlike in the Byzantine and Mozarabic traditions, where it serves as a profession of the orthodox faith in every eucharistic celebration.

11

Reform Papacy and Liturgical Unification

As the papal reform movement was gaining momentum in the course of the eleventh century, the papacy resumed its leading role in the development of the Roman Rite. Gregory VII (r. 1073–1085) was crucial in this process—not, however, because of a far-reaching liturgical agenda (which he did not have), but rather because of his theological and canonical initiatives that set the tone for things to come.

Liturgy in the Pontificate of Gregory VII

A good source for Gregory VII's liturgical ideas is Bernold of Constance, who stayed in Rome from 1079 to 1084 and between 1086 and 1090 and wrote a commentary on the Mass known as *Micrologus de ecclesiasticis observationibus*, a work that subsequently enjoyed considerable circulation and influence. Bernold reports the pope's interest in studying apostolic traditions and his aim of restoring what was held to be Roman use in the age of Gregory the Great.[1] Against this backdrop, it may appear ironic that

[1] Bernold of Constance, *Micrologus de ecclesiasticis observationibus* 5, 14, 17, 43, 56.

the Mass "iuxtam Romanam consuetudinem" (according to the Roman custom),[2] which Bernold expounds in the *Micrologus*, shows that the Rhenish *Ordo Missae* tradition had become an integral part of the rite followed by the pope and his curia. However, despite his repeated insistence on Roman custom (*consuetudo*), manner (*mos*), authority (*auctoritas*), and order (*ordo*), Bernold was not a naïve observer, and he was aware that not all of the prayers used at Mass were of Roman origin—for instance, the Gallican invocation of the Holy Spirit, *Veni, sanctificator* ("Come, O Sanctifier"), at the offertory.

The *Micrologus* reports with disapproval that during the Canon some priests interpolate prayers in the commemoration of the living (*Memento, Domine*) and of the dead (*Memento etiam, Domine*). Priests who insert the Incarnation into the anamnestic section of *Unde et memories* and extend the lists of the saints are likewise censured.[3] Bernold thus witnesses to the increasing insistence on the written ritual, as well as to priests being inclined to add to the received text.

A committed advocate for the Gregorian reform, Bernold does not seem to be overly concerned with establishing the "purely" Roman tradition, but rather with following the liturgical order of the contemporary papacy. Thus, the *Micrologus* echoes the policy of Gregory VII, who demanded that the Roman Rite, purged of recently introduced German customs, should be the norm for the whole Latin Church. Still, the pope enacted only very minor liturgical changes to implement this demand. Thus, the liturgical sources of the Gregorian period show the continued impact of the Romano-Germanic tradition.

[2] Ibid., 1; see also the brief description of a priest's Mass in ibid., 23.
[3] Ibid., 13.

However, the strong claim for papal authority, epitomized in the *Dictatus papae*,[4] was of long-term consequences for the Western Church in general and for the ordering of its divine worship in particular. Moreover, the (then-largely rhetorical) emphasis on investigating apostolic traditions and restoring the purity of ancient Roman observance helped create a mentality that was to have a lasting effect on conceptions of liturgical renewal.

Of immediate impact were the calls for local churches to follow Roman customs and observances, in order to guarantee doctrinal purity and ecclesiastical unity. Reform popes before Gregory VII had already made such demands in Italy with regard to the Ambrosian tradition in the North and the Beneventan tradition in the South. While Gregory refused to concede the use of the Slavonic language in territories he claimed for the Latin Church (Croatia and Bohemia), he did not insist on liturgical conformity in relation to the Greek and Armenian churches. Regarding Eastern Christianity, his main concern was a recognition of the primacy of the papacy.[5]

In continuity with his immediate predecessors, Gregory VII was persistent in his efforts to have the Hispanic (Mozarabic) Rite replaced by the Roman Rite throughout the Iberian Peninsula, with the intention of binding the reconquered Christian territories to the See of Rome and forging the unity of Latin Christendom. This momentous change had been initiated in the Kingdom of Aragón in the pontificate of Alexander II (r. 1061–1073) through the activities of his legate Cardinal Hugh of Remiremont, and it was facilitated by Cluniac influence on monasteries in

[4] The *Dictatus papae* is a list of twenty-seven brief statements of papal power, which are included in the register of letters of Gregory VII for the year 1075.

[5] See H.E.J. Cowdrey, "Pope Gregory VII (1073–85) and the Liturgy", *Journal of Theological Studies*, n.s., 55 (2004): 79–81.

northern Spain. Gregory's campaign was crowned with success when at the Council of Burgos in May 1080, King Alfonso VI of León and Castile decided to adopt the Roman Rite in his realm.[6] However, the substitution was not complete, and the Mozarabic liturgy continued to be celebrated in some places, especially in Toledo, its traditional center, which Alfonso took in 1085.[7]

Liturgical Variety in the City of Rome

Present-day historians are inclined to highlight elements of diversity and innovation, and historians of the liturgy make no exception to this trend. However, it needs to be recognized that there are significant differences in the evolution of liturgical forms and genres. For instance, Mary C. Mansfield notes:

> Undoubtedly some rites hardly altered over many centuries. The canon of the mass, to take the most obvious example, remained stable because of its central importance from ancient times. Generally, as one moved outward from the canon first to the rest of the liturgy of the mass, then to the daily office, and finally to occasional rites like penance, one finds at each step more tolerance for alteration.[8]

The core of the eucharistic liturgy, inherited from its formative period between the fifth and the seventh centuries,

[6] See ibid., 78–79.

[7] See Ludwig Vones, "The Substitution of the Hispanic Liturgy by the Roman Rite in the Kingdoms of the Iberian Peninsula", in *Hispania Vetus: Musical-Liturgical Manuscripts: From Visigothic Origins to the Franco-Roman Transition, 9th–12th Centuries*, ed. Susana Zapke (Bilbao: Fundación BBVA, 2007), 43–59.

[8] Mary C. Mansfield, *The Humiliation of Sinners: Public Penance in Thirteenth-century France* (Ithaca, NY, and London: Cornell University Press, 1995), 160.

showed remarkable continuity throughout the Middle Ages. Local variations concerned more peripheral aspects of the celebration of Mass, such as the choice of readings or the sanctoral calendar. Nonetheless, the importance of ritual in medieval society ensured that such disparities could provoke tension and even conflict.[9]

Within the stable framework established by the rite of Mass, there was no strict uniformity in particular ceremonies and observances even within the city of Rome. The Lateran Basilica, the cathedral of the pope as bishop of Rome, which held the title "mother and head of all the churches in the city and the world" (*omnium urbis et orbis ecclesiarum mater et caput*), had no claim to impose its use on the many churches and monasteries of the city, and certainly not on St. Peter's in the Vatican, its rival for honor and prestige. At the time, the cycle of papal stational Masses was still a living reality, and proper customs (as well as local prerogatives) were maintained with tenacity.[10]

The Gregorian reform strengthened the power and prestige of the papal curia (often rendered "household" or "court"), and gradually the papal chapel, rather than the Lateran Basilica, became the model for liturgical observance in Rome and beyond.[11] The curial liturgy was conducted with solemnity, especially in the splendid thirteenth-century setting of the chapel of St. Lawrence in the Lateran Palace, known as the Sancta Sanctorum for

[9] See Vittorio Peri, "'*Nichil in ecclesia sine causa': Note di vita liturgica romana nel XII secolo*", *Rivista di archeologia cristiana* 50 (1974): 249–73, on the uncompromisingly conservative attitude of the Roman deacon Nicola Magnacozza (Latinized: Maniacutius) in the twelfth century.

[10] See Cowdrey, "Pope Gregory VII and the Liturgy", 57–58.

[11] See Stephen J. P. van Dijk, O.F.M., and Joan Hazelden Walker, *The Origins of the Modern Roman Liturgy: The Liturgy of the Papal Court and the Franciscan Order in the Thirteenth Century* (Westminster, MD: Newman Press; London: Darton, Longman & Todd, 1960), 80–87.

its outstanding collection of relics. Beginning with the pontificate of Innocent III (r. 1198–1216), popes increasingly used the Vatican palace as a residence and its "great chapel" (*capella magna*) for liturgical celebrations. However, these ceremonial spaces were relatively small and did not allow for the processional elements that characterized stational liturgies in the churches of the city. Moreover, the papal court often traveled in this period, and, for reasons of expediency, the curia's liturgical use was given a standard form that could also be transferred to places with fewer resources, such as Anagni or Orvieto.

Still, the impact of the papal chapel remained geographically limited, and general conformity with Roman liturgical practice began to be observed throughout the Latin Church only with the rapid expansion of the new Franciscan Order in the thirteenth century.

12

The Impact of the Franciscans on the Roman Mass

The mendicant orders, such as the Franciscans and Dominicans, constituted a new type of religious life without a vow of stability, as taken by monks. With Latin as the common language of the Church, of higher education and culture, the friars enjoyed considerable mobility throughout Europe. It proved onerous for them to adapt to local liturgical variations, and so the desire arose for a unified practice within the orders. After an initial period of diversity, the Dominicans adopted a proper use of the Roman Rite that was established in 1256 by the Master of the Order, Humbert de Romans.[1] The Franciscans accepted the liturgical books of the Roman Rite in the form used by the papal curia.

Indutus Planeta

A momentous step in the history of Roman Mass liturgy is the work of Haymo of Faversham, who served as Franciscan minister general from 1240 until his death in 1244.

[1] See the still valid work of William R. Bonniwell, *A History of the Dominican Liturgy 1215–1945*, 2nd ed. revised and enlarged (New York: Joseph F. Wagner, 1945).

At the order's chapter in Bologna in 1243, Haymo presented the ordinal known by its opening words *Indutus planeta* ("Wearing the chasuble ..."), which describes itself as an "ordo agendorum et dicendorum"—that is, an order regulating the ceremonies to be carried out and the texts to be recited, specifically for the private Mass of a priest or the simple conventual Mass on a ferial day.[2] *Indutus planeta* was based on the use of the papal curia; it was adopted by the Friars Minor and helped to create a unified liturgy in the mendicant order.

For the introductory rites and the offertory rites (except for a few ceremonial details), the document set the pattern that was to become normative in the Roman Mass until the reforms of the 1960s. The priest's physical postures and gestures are described with attention to detail, especially for the Canon. The comprehensive instructions of *Indutus planeta* in turn influenced the liturgical practice of the papal curia and helped to shape the *Ordo missalis secundum consuetudinem Romane curie*, which was gradually incorporated into missals of local dioceses and religious orders throughout Europe. Thus, through the agency of the Franciscans, a unification of the ritual structure and shape of the Mass was achieved in the Latin Church to a degree that previous popes may have demanded but were never able to implement effectively. Needless to say, such standardization of the missal (and the breviary), for which the Franciscans acted as a catalyst, did not happen overnight, but through a long and complex process of manuscript transmission. Local variations remained, especially in the introductory, offertory, and concluding rites.

[2] A critical edition of *Indutus planeta* is included in *Sources of the Modern Roman Liturgy: The Ordinals by Haymo of Faversham and Related Documents, 1243–1307*, ed. Stephen J.P. van Dijk, 2 vols., Studia et documenta franciscana 1–2 (Leiden: Brill, 1963), 2:1–14.

The Plenary Missal and the Expansion of Private Masses

Between the ninth and the thirteenth centuries, manuscripts compiled and arranged for distinct liturgical actors (sacramentary, lectionary, antiphoner) were gradually supplanted by manuscripts containing the complete texts of a particular ritual celebration (pontifical, missal, breviary). This process of transition was anything but uniform and needs to be considered separately for each genre of liturgical book.

The plenary missal (*liber missalis*, *missale*) came into being for largely practical reasons. Cathedrals, monasteries, and collegiate churches could easily muster the human and material resources for the solemn celebration of the liturgy, including the set of books for distinct clerical functions. But as the network of parish churches was growing even in remote areas of northern and western Europe, Mass was frequently celebrated in modest circumstances that would permit only a simpler form of the rite. A single manuscript that contains all the texts of the Mass, which is first attested in the ninth century, proved to be pastorally useful. The popularity of the plenary missal was also facilitated by the growing practice of "private Masses", which led to the concentration of liturgical roles in the person of the offering priest. However, Stephen van Dijk and Joan Hazelden Walker rightly caution that the relationship between the two phenomena is not as straightforward as is often assumed.[3] There is considerable variety in Mass books between the ninth and the twelfth century: some sacramentaries are supplied with marginal notes to indicate the incipits of chants (presumably sung from

[3] Stephen J. P. van Dijk, O.F.M., and Joan Hazelden Walker, *The Origins of the Modern Roman Liturgy: The Liturgy of the Papal Court and the Franciscan Order in the Thirteenth Century* (Westminster, MD: Newman Press; London: Darton, Longman & Todd, 1960), 57–66.

memory); some manuscripts represent a full sacramentary-gradual, and in some cases a lectionary is added so that all the Mass texts are contained in one book, though in separate sections. Moreover, the regular offering of votive Masses did not require a plenary missal with the full cycle of the liturgical year; a modest fascicle (*libellus missarum*) with the specific texts would be sufficient.

Small gatherings for the Eucharist are attested in the first three centuries, when Christian communities found themselves in a vulnerable position and subject to occasional persecutions. Such circumstances demanded a simplicity of external ritual, which continued in places where congregations were small and resources were limited. However, the private Mass of the early medieval period is not just defined by its simplicity of ritual. The novelty consisted in the celebration of Mass by a priest with only one or two assistants; unlike in conventual or parochial Masses, the participation of the lay faithful would be merely accidental. From the fourth century onward, there is growing evidence for the frequent, even daily offering of the Eucharist in the Latin West, which is associated with the ascetical movement. The devout ideal of each priest celebrating Mass daily for the spiritual benefit of the living and the dead became prevalent, and it was probably the general rule in monasteries by the eighth century. Another important factor needs to be considered—namely, the laity's growing desire to have Masses offered for specific intentions (*vota*), which had its roots in late antiquity. Of particular significance was the increasing demand for Masses for the dead, especially on fixed days for memorials.

Secular priests followed the monastic example and began to offer Mass more often, sometimes even several times a day, to fulfill particular Mass intentions (for which it was customary to offer a stipend). This practice was repeatedly censured in ecclesiastical legislation, until Innocent III in

1206 definitely limited the number of Masses a priest could offer to one a day, except on Christmas Day (where the Roman tradition lists three papal Masses in different stational churches) and in case of necessity. In the ninth and tenth centuries, bishops and synods also repeatedly prohibited the *missa solitaria*—that is, the priest's offering of Mass with no attendants at all. Even a private Mass should be celebrated with the assistance of one or two clerics in minor orders (in accordance with the plural form of the liturgical salutation "Dominus vobiscum").[4]

In the private celebration of Mass, the parts assigned in its solemn form to distinct liturgical ministries were recited by the priest himself, and they were increasingly spoken rather than chanted. As the space on side altars was smaller, the ceremonial was reduced and eventually the lessons were read by the priest at the altar. The ascendancy of private Masses seems gradually to have given rise to the custom, first attested in the ordo of the Lateran Basilica dating from the mid-twelfth century, that in the solemn Mass the celebrant would recite in a low voice the Ordinary and Proper chants that were sung by the schola, as well as the readings proclaimed by the subdeacon and deacon.

While deploring this development, which separates the priest from the schola cantorum and facilitates the secularization of church music, Josef Andreas Jungmann caustically remarks that there is some progress in the fact that the priest, instead of filling every available moment with lengthy *apologiae*, actually recites the biblical texts of the Mass Propers.[5] In fact, the new practice might have been

[4] See Andreas Amiet, "Die liturgische Gesetzgebung der deutschen Reichskirche in der Zeit der sächsischen Kaiser 922–1023", *Zeitschrift für schweizerische Kirchengeschichte* 70 (1976): 21–24.

[5] Josef A. Jungmann, *The Mass of the Roman Rite: Its Origins and Development (Missarum Sollemnia)*, trans. Francis A. Brunner, 2 vols. (New York: Benziger, 1951), 1:106–7.

motivated by the desire to curb the priest's private prayers and to align them with the official liturgical texts. Notwithstanding the strong impact of the private Mass, the solemn Mass (*missa solemnis*) with the assistance of deacon and subdeacon remained the normative form of the rite. Thirteenth-century theological treatises on the liturgy, including the writings of Saint Thomas Aquinas,[6] naturally comment on the solemn Mass.

[6] Thomas Aquinas, *Super sent.*, lib. 4, d. 8, q. 2, a. 4, qc. 3 expos.; *Summa theologiae* III, q. 83, a. 4 co.

13

Eucharistic Devotion of the High Middle Ages

The interplay of doctrinal clarification and popular devotion in the medieval period led to a heightened sense of the Real Presence of Christ in the Mass.[1] Kneeling during the Eucharistic Prayer had become increasingly common among the laity since the ninth century. Starting from France, possibly as a reaction to the Albigensian denial of incarnational and sacramental reality, priests would elevate the consecrated Host for the adoration of the faithful, after pronouncing the words of Christ over it. The practice was confirmed by the bishop of Paris, Odo of Sully (d. 1208), and in the course of the thirteenth century, the elevation of the consecrated chalice was likewise introduced. The elevations could be accompanied by a special candle, by the ringing of a handbell or even by the tolling of the church bells. Saint Francis of Assisi (d. 1226) promoted these new forms of eucharistic devotion enthusiastically and strongly encouraged the lay

[1] See the excellent overview of Helmut Hoping, *My Body Given for You: History and Theology of the Eucharist*, trans. Michael J. Miller (San Francisco: Ignatius Press, 2019), 175–210.

faithful to kneel at the elevation of the consecrated species at Mass and when the Blessed Sacrament is carried in procession.[2]

Reception of Communion

Fourth- and fifth-century sources indicate that, by that period, the reception of Communion by the laity had already become less frequent than in former times. Some Carolingian bishops encouraged the faithful to receive the sacrament more often, but these efforts had little apparent success, and ecclesiastical legislation largely followed the pattern set by the Council of Agde in the south of France, held in 506, which obliged general Communion three times a year, at Christmas, Easter, and Pentecost.[3] The people's vivid faith in Christ's presence in the eucharistic species and the sense of their own sinfulness made the reception of Communion a rare occasion. The Fourth Lateran Council in 1215 even saw the need to legislate that the faithful had to receive the sacrament at least once a year in the Easter season ("in pascha").[4] By that time, the chalice was no longer given to the laity in most churches of the West, and since the eighth or ninth century, a thin wafer of unleavened bread, made of water and wheat, had

[2] See Augustine Thompson, *Francis of Assisi: A New Biography* (Ithaca, NY: Cornell University Press, 2012), 62, 83–86.

[3] See Andreas Amiet, "Die liturgische Gesetzgebung der deutschen Reichskirche in der Zeit der sächsischen Kaiser 922–1023", *Zeitschrift für schweizerische Kirchengeschichte* 70 (1976): 82–84.

[4] Fourth Lateran Council, *Constitutiones*, 21. *De confessione facienda et non revelanda a sacerdote et saltem in pascha communicandos* (30 novembre 1215), in *Enchiridion symbolorum definitionum et declarationum de rebus fidei et morum*, ed. Heinrich Denzinger et Peter Hünermann, 43rd ed. (San Francisco: Ignatius Press, 2012), no. 812.

become the norm.[5] From the eleventh century, the use of Hosts that were consecrated in another Mass began to spread. Until then, this practice was limited to the Mass of the Presanctified on Good Friday, when the sacrament that had been confected on Maundy Thursday was distributed. If at a Mass consecrated Hosts were left over, they were ordinarily consumed by the priest. The administration of Holy Communion outside Mass is first attested in the twelfth century. Until the sixteenth century, this seemed to happen only at Easter and other major feasts when there were many communicants, and the sacrament was distributed right after Mass so as to maintain a connection with the offering of the sacrifice.[6]

Reservation of the Eucharist

The reservation of the Eucharist to make it available to the sick and the dying has its roots in Christian antiquity. The *conditorium* mentioned in *Ordo Romanus I*[7] probably means a cupboard or chest kept in the sacristy (a custom maintained in northern Italy, including Milan Cathedral, until the sixteenth century). In the early medieval period, it was

[5] There is some evidence for the use of unleavened bread in the Eucharist from the Christian East in the late sixth century. This has been the practice of the Armenian church since at least the synod of Dvin in 719 and may go back to the seventh century. See Jean Michel Hanssens, *Institutiones liturgicae de ritibus orientalibus, Tomus II: De missa rituum orientalium, Pars prima* (Rome: Apud Aedes Pont. Universitatis Gregorianae, 1930), 133–41.

[6] On these and related questions, see the outstanding contributions of Peter Browe, which have been republished in the volume *Die Eucharistie im Mittelalter: Liturgiehistorische Forschungen in kulturwissenschaftlicher Absicht*, ed. Hubertus Lutterbach and Thomas Flammer, Vergessene Theologen 1, 7th ed. (Münster: Lit Verlag, 2019).

[7] *Ordo Romanus I*, 48.

established to keep the consecrated Hosts in churches, to protect them from profanation, and to prevent superstitious practices, and various places and forms of reservation are attested. The ordinal of the Dominican Missal of 1256 and the ceremonial *ordinationes* of the Augustinian friars of 1290 stipulate that the sacrament is to be reserved on the high altar (*altare maius*). The common source for the practice of these orders (there is apparently no similarly precise indication in contemporary Franciscan documents) may well be the papal chapel, where the sacrament was customarily (though with exceptions) kept at the high altar.[8] From the late thirteenth century, the word *tabernaculum* ("tabernacle" or "tent") was employed to indicate the receptacle for the sacrament of the altar. The biblical associations of the term are significant, since the Tent of Meeting was God's presence among the people of Israel in the desert. The prologue of Saint John's Gospel states that the divine "Word was made flesh and dwelt [literally, pitched his tent] among us" (1:14). In the Book of Revelation, the heavenly Jerusalem is evoked with the words "Behold, the dwelling of God is with men", which reads in the Vulgate: "Ecce tabernaculum Dei cum hominibus" (21:3).

Corpus Christi

Medieval veneration of the Eucharist reached its climax with the introduction of the Feast of Corpus Christi and the forms of popular devotion associated with it: procession, exposition, and benediction of the Blessed Sacrament.

[8] See Stephen J. P. van Dijk, O.F.M., and Joan Hazelden Walker, *The Origins of the Modern Roman Liturgy: The Liturgy of the Papal Court and the Franciscan Order in the Thirteenth Century* (Westminster, MD: Newman Press; London: Darton, Longman & Todd, 1960), 369–70.

The proximate origins of Corpus Christi are connected with the visions of Saint Juliana (d. 1258), a lay sister serving in a *leprosarium* (leper house) connected with the Premonstratensian house of Mont-Cornillon near Liège.[9] The idea of a new liturgical feast dedicated to the Eucharist resonated widely and was promoted especially by the Dominicans, and its observance spread through the Low Countries and Germany. Jacques Pantaleon, archdeacon of Campines in the Diocese of Liège and a great supporter of Juliana, became pope as Urban IV (r. 1261–1264), and in his bull *Transiturus* of 1264 decreed the celebration of Corpus Christi for the whole Church on the Thursday after Trinity Sunday. The date was chosen to connect the new feast with Maundy Thursday, when the Institution of the Eucharist is commemorated, and it was in fact the first available Thursday after the conclusion of the Easter season. Recent research has confirmed the traditional ascription of the Mass and Office for Corpus Christi to Saint Thomas Aquinas.[10]

Urban IV died shortly after *Transiturus* and his immediate successors seemed to have little interest in the new feast; nonetheless, its celebration spread throughout the Western Church, thanks to the initiatives of local bishops and religious orders, and in northern Europe it was particularly associated with processions of the Blessed Sacrament. The first Corpus Christi procession is attested in Cologne between 1265 and 1277. At this early stage, the consecrated Host was carried in a closed pyxis, but soon a monstrance or ostensory (from the Latin *monstrare* or *ostendere*,

[9] On the institution of the feast, see Miri Rubin, *Corpus Christi: The Eucharist in Late Medieval Culture* (Cambridge: Cambridge University Press, 1991), 164–99.

[10] See Jean-Pierre Torrell, *Saint Thomas Aquinas*, vol. 1, *The Person and His Work*, trans. Robert Royal (Washington, DC: The Catholic University of America Press, 1996), 129–36.

which both mean "to show") with a glass frame was used that exposed the sacrament for the adoration of the people. The universal observance of the feast was renewed by the Avignon Pope John XXII (r. 1316–1334) in 1317, when he promulgated the collection of canon law authorized by his predecessor Clement V (r. 1305–1314) and known as the *Clementine Constitutions* (*Constitutiones clementinae*).

The impact of the new feast on later medieval society can hardly be overestimated. Miri Rubin's acclaimed study offers a lively account of how Corpus Christi "became the central symbol of a culture"[11] that was almost universally shared in Western Christendom until the Protestant Reformation.

[11] Rubin, *Corpus Christi*, 347.

14

The Later Middle Ages: All Decay and Decline?

Standard liturgical textbooks have tended to dismiss the later medieval period as marked by decline and disintegration. The Mass, it is argued, had developed into an almost exclusively clerical exercise of an overgrown ritual system in an incomprehensible language. Consequently, lay participation largely disappeared, including the reception of Holy Communion. The faithful would rather occupy themselves with private devotions.[1] This reading has fed the general narrative of a Church in crisis that almost inevitably led to the Protestant Reformation of the sixteenth century. In recent decades, however, historians have offered new perspectives on Christianity in the later Middle Ages and have highlighted that elements of decline and vitality existed side by side. In liturgical scholarship, the traditional focus on texts is now enriched by multidisciplinary studies of late medieval worship from musical, artistic, literary, social, and more general religious perspectives.

[1] See, for example, the devastating assessment of Anscar J. Chupungco, "History of the Roman Liturgy until the Fifteenth Century", in *Handbook for Liturgical Studies*, vol. 1, *Introduction to the Liturgy*, ed. Anscar J. Chupungco (Collegeville, MN: Liturgical Press, 1997), 150.

The prevailing use of Latin as a sacred language certainly removed the liturgy from the vast majority of the lay faithful, but it did not raise an impenetrable barrier to popular participation, as is often assumed. At least in Romance-speaking countries, where the vernacular language developed from Latin, there was a basic understanding at least of the meaning conveyed in liturgical texts.[2] Moreover, the vernacular prayer of the faithful at the main Sunday Mass in the parish church offered to the laity a form of involvement that corresponded to their spiritual and temporal needs. The oldest known example of such "bidding prayers" from England precedes the Norman Conquest and has been dated to the early eleventh century. The prayer of the faithful employed regional languages, such as Catalan, Basque, and Breton, as well as Occitan and German dialects.[3] This vernacular rite was inserted at some point during the offertory, and commonly after the incensation of the gifts and the altar and before the priest's washing of hands (*lavabo*).

Liturgical participation cannot be reduced to the comprehension of texts, and Frank Senn has proposed a broader conception that includes "other 'vernaculars' than language,

[2] See Augustine Thompson, *Cities of God: The Religion of the Italian Communes 1125–1325* (University Park, PA: The Pennsylvania State University Press, 2005), 239–41.

[3] Jean-Baptiste Molin has published collections of medieval formularies in various European languages in "L'*oratio communis fidelium* au Moyen Âge en Occident du Xe au XVe siècle", in *Miscellanea liturgica in onore di Sua Eminenza il Cardinale Giacomo Lercaro*, 2 vols. (Rome: Desclée, 1966–1967), 2:315–468, and "Quelques textes médiévaux de la prière universelle", in *Traditio et Progressio: Studi liturgici in onore del Prof. Adrien Nocent, OSB*, ed. Giustino Farnedi, Studia Anselmiana 95, Analecta liturgica 12 (Rome: Pontificio Ateneo S. Anselmo, 1988), 338–58.

not least of which were the church buildings themselves and the liturgical art that decorated them".[4] From a similar perspective, Éric Palazzo has explored the sensory dimensions of the liturgy: the stimulation of seeing, hearing, smelling, touching, and tasting made participation in the Mass a synesthetic experience.[5] Lay participation was by its very nature unscripted: it was not regulated by the official liturgical books that gave detailed instructions to the clergy regarding what to say and how to perform the sacred rites. Thus, the faithful were able to engage with the Mass in a variety of ways that are not easy for us to grasp precisely because they were not scripted. Paul S. Barnwell speaks of "the meditative and affective nature of much lay devotion in the period".[6] The sensory dimensions of the late medieval liturgy offered important stimuli for such meditation. The faithful who attended Mass weekly (and many of them daily) would be familiar with the stable parts of the Ordinary. It is worth noting that the laity found the parish Mass celebrated at the high altar less approachable, since they were at considerable physical distance from the priest and their view was restricted not only by the rood screen but also by servers and singers in the chancel. "Private" Masses at a side altar offered a more direct way for the faithful to engage with the liturgical action both visually and aurally, and this contributed to their popularity. Woodcut representations of the Mass in moral and

[4] Frank C. Senn, *The People's Work: A Social History of the Liturgy* (Minneapolis: Fortress Press, 2006), 145.

[5] Éric Palazzo, "Art, Liturgy and the Five Senses in the Early Middle Ages", *Viator* 41 (2010): 25–56.

[6] Paul S. Barnwell, "How to Do without Rubrics: Experiments in Reconstructing Medieval Lay Experience", in *Late Medieval Liturgies Enacted: The Experience of Worship in Cathedral and Parish Church*, ed. Sally Harper, Paul S. Barnwell, and Magnus Williamson (London and New York: Routledge, 2016), 238.

devotional literature from the period show lay men and women in close proximity to the priest at a side altar of a church.[7]

The "vernaculars" other than language, evoked by Senn, spoke eloquently to worshippers both as private individuals and—in a juxtaposition typical of the religious practice of the later Middle Ages—as a body. To quote an influential essay by the historian John Bossy, the Mass was a "social institution"[8] and created a bond that not only was expressed verbally through praying for one another, but became tangible in two particular rites: in the giving of the peace by kissing and passing the tablet known as pax, pax-brede, or *pacificale*, and in the distribution of blessed bread after the Mass. Both rites can be understood as substitutes for sacramental Communion, which for most laypeople did not extend beyond the annual reception at Easter as prescribed by Lateran IV, but at the same time expressed the community-building power of the liturgy.

Preaching at Mass

There is scarce evidence from the post-Carolingian period for preaching in a liturgical context. This does not mean that there was no proclamation of the Gospel and transmission of the faith; however, Christian teaching was

[7] See Gabriela Signori, *Räume, Gesten, Andachtsformen: Geschlecht, Konflikt und religiöse Kultur im europäischen Mittelalter* (Ostfildern: Jan Thorbecke Verlag, 2005), 43, 70.

[8] John Bossy, "The Mass as a Social Institution, 1200–1700", *Past & Present*, no. 100 (August 1983): 29–61; see also Thompson, "The City Worships", in *Cities of God*, 235–71, and Eamon Duffy, "The Mass", in *The Stripping of the Altars: Traditional Religion in England 1400–1570*, 2nd ed. (New Haven, CT, and London: Yale University Press, 2005), 91–130.

embedded in a culture that was largely oral, and it was not considered an integral part of the Church's public worship, which relied on a written text.[9] From the twelfth century, however, preaching is given increasing importance in both liturgical and canonical sources. While sermons could be given on various occasions, some of them extraliturgical, they acquire a stable place in pontifical celebrations. The ordo of the papal Mass established by Gregory X (r. 1271–1276) includes a sermon by the pope after the Gospel, partly in Latin and partly in the vernacular, which is followed by a general confession, (nonsacramental) absolution, and a blessing.[10] In the pontifical of William Durandus, written between 1292 and 1295, the bishop's preaching is particularly associated with such a penitential rite, to which indulgences are attached.[11] This practice was soon adopted in the Mass celebrated by a priest.

Parish priests throughout Europe were expected to preach on Sundays and major feast days.[12] Not all of them may have been sufficiently trained to do so, and not all of them may have fulfilled their duty conscientiously, but in general, preaching was popular among the ordinary faithful. North of the Alps, benefices were founded for secular priests to exercise the office of preacher (*Prädikatur*) from

[9] See R. Emmet McLaughlin, "The Word Eclipsed? Preaching in the Early Middle Ages", *Traditio* 46 (1991): 77–122.

[10] *Ordinal of Gregory X (c. 1274)*, in *The Ordinal of the Papal Court from Innocent III to Boniface VIII and Related Documents*, ed. Stephen J. P. van Dijk and Joan Hazelden Walker, Spicilegium Friburgense 22 (Fribourg, Switzerland: University Press, 1975), 586.

[11] William Durandus, *Pontificale* III.18.34, ed. Michel Andrieu, *Le pontifical romain au Moyen-Âge*, Studi e testi 88 (Vatican City: Biblioteca Apostolica Vaticana, 1940), 3:639.

[12] See Thompson, *Cities of God*, 251, 335–37, for northern Italy; McLaughlin, "Word Eclipsed?", 77, for Germany; Duffy, *Stripping of the Altars*, 57–58, for England.

the late fourteenth century and especially in the second half of the fifteenth century. The importance of regular sermons was widely recognized and was promoted by the conciliarist reform movement.

In sum, liturgical practice in the later medieval period offers a complex picture, but it was not all decay and decline. The Church's sacramental system remained remarkably resilient and was deeply rooted in the people's cycle of life.

15

The Rite of Mass at the Eve of the Protestant Reformation

At the dawn of early modernity, while a variety of diocesan and religious uses persisted, the *Ordo Missae* after the model of the Roman Curia had been widely adopted throughout the Western Church. The tendency toward codification of ritual culminated in Johann Burchard's detailed ordo of 1502, which became influential in the period leading up to the Council of Trent.

Unity and Diversity in the Development of the Missal

The later Middle Ages witnessed a liturgical standardization according to the model of the Roman Curia, which increasingly shaped local diocesan uses. Despite such tendencies toward unification, variations in the missals of dioceses and religious orders remained and were noteworthy in certain respects: in the formal presentation of liturgical formularies (such as the names for the Mass Propers); in the prayers, readings, and chants assigned to feasts; in the sanctoral cycle of the calendar; and in the structure and sequence of sections within the missal. Even where the Order of Mass essentially followed the use of the Roman Curia (*Ordo missalis secundum consuetudinem Romane curie*), there were differences in the texts and rubrics of the introductory and the concluding rites. Likewise, the ritual shape and the prayers of the offertory were by no means uniform. Liturgical diversification increased with the addition of new saints' feasts, the proliferation of Prefaces, tropes, and sequences (of uneven quality), and the multiplication of votive Masses.

In general, diocesan bishops did not have effective control over the making of liturgical books in their territories. Before the invention of printing, manuscripts for liturgical use were usually copied at the initiative of local churches and their clergy, who would engage scribes for this particular purpose.[1] Local nobility or other patrons would often donate missals and be involved in their production. Episcopal leadership was mostly reactive, and its limits are illustrated by the largely unsuccessful efforts of Nicholas of Cusa, who as bishop of Brixen tried to enforce the correction of missals in use according to approved normative manuscripts at two diocesan synods in 1453 and 1455.[2] The new, fast-growing, and largely unregulated printing industry dramatically simplified the production of liturgical books and gave printers an important role in this process. Printers would confidently supply their editions with Mass formularies that corresponded to devotions popular at the time, perhaps with the collaboration and the advice of local clergy.

Codification of Ritual

The move of the papacy to Avignon in 1309 brought the cycle of stational liturgies in Rome to a definite halt. In

[1] Natalia Nowakowska, "From Strassburg to Trent: Bishops, Printing and Liturgical Reform in the Fifteenth Century", *Past & Present*, no. 213 (November 2011): 24, points to the evidence provided by contracts from fifteenth-century Poland and England.

[2] See Hubert Jedin, "Das Konzil von Trient und die Reform des Römischen Meßbuches", *Liturgisches Leben* 6 (1939): 40–41.

Avignon, papal liturgical celebrations were also held in the setting of the palace. Even after the return of the pope to Rome in 1378 and the end of the Western Schism in 1417, the intimate link of the papal liturgy with the urban churches was never resumed.[3] The Vatican palace became the pope's preferred residence, and major liturgical celebrations were held in its "great chapel" (*capella magna*), known as the Sistine Chapel since its rebuilding under Pope Sixtus IV (r. 1471–1484).

As the conciliarist movement diminished because of its failure to deliver its stated program of renewing the Church "in head and members", the papacy regained momentum, and its liturgical celebrations once again began to be imitated by bishops throughout the Latin Church. The papal masters of ceremonies Agostino Patrizi Piccolomini (d. 1495), Johann Burchard (d. 1506), and Paride Grassi (d. 1528), also referred to by his Latinized name, Paris de Grassis, were responsible for organizing both liturgy and court ceremonial and left extensive written records of their work (prescriptive ceremonial books, descriptive diaries, and treatises).

These masters of ceremonies were working in a tradition going back to the *Ordines Romani* of the early medieval period. From the late thirteenth century onward, ceremonial instructions became more systematic and specific, and they had considerable impact beyond their immediate purpose throughout the Latin Church.[4] The work was to become decisive for the further development

[3] See John F. Romano, "Innocent II and the Liturgy", in *Pope Innocent II (1130–43): The World vs the City*, ed. John Doran and Damian J. Smith, Church, Faith and Culture in the Medieval West (Abingdon and New York: Routledge, 2016), 344–45.

[4] The papal ceremonials have been edited by Marc Dykmans, S.J., *Le cérémonial papal de la fin du Moyen-Âge à la Renaissance*, 4 vols., Bibliothèque de l'Institut Historique Belge de Rome 24–27 (Brussels and Rome: Institut Historique Belge de Rome, 1977–1985).

of the ritual shape of the Roman Mass, the *Ordo Missae* of Johann Burchard. The first edition of 1496 is presented as an "Order to be observed by a priest in the celebration of Mass without chant and without ministers according to the rite of the holy Roman church", which is compiled for the purpose of "the instruction of newly ordained priests".[5] The scope of the second edition, printed in 1502 with a letter of approval from Pope Alexander VI, is much broader than its predecessor: Burchard insists that its ceremonial instructions also apply to cardinals and prelates, including the pope, when they celebrate Mass not pontifically but in private.[6]

The papal master of ceremonies thoroughly reworked his earlier ordo for the new edition, which offers much more detailed and comprehensive rubrical instructions. Now the ritual performance of gestures and movements is precisely regulated and meticulously explained. By contrast, the *Ordinarium Missae* (named after its incipit "Paratus sacerdos"), which was integrated into the Roman Missal and contained the recurring parts of the rite, was largely limited to prayer texts and had room only for very few rubrics. Thus, the ordo of 1502 can be best understood in continuity with the thirteenth-century ordinal *Indutus planeta*. Burchard offers important specifications at three stages of the rite: First, in the introductory rites, Psalm 42 (*Iudica me*) is recited at the foot of the altar (which was Roman practice at least since *Indutus planeta*), rather than

[5]Johann Burchard, *Ordo missae secundum consuetudinem Romanae ecclesiae* (Rome: Andreas Fritag and Johann Besicken, 1496). The slightly altered 1498 reprint has been digitized by the Biblioteca Apostolica Vaticana and is accessible at https://digi.vatlib.it/view/Inc.IV.528.

[6]Johann Burchard, *Ordo Missae* (Rome: Johannes Besicken, 1502); cited after *Tracts on the Mass*, ed. John Wickham Legg, Henry Bradshaw Society 27 (London: Harrison, 1904), 126.

in the sacristy or in procession to the sanctuary, as was common in diocesan uses. Second, while the offertory rite is fixed in its curial form, the 1502 ordo (but not the earlier edition) includes an offertory procession, which still had some currency at the time. Third, in the concluding rites, the final blessing follows after the prayer *Placeat tibi sancta Trinitas* ("May it please you, O holy Trinity ..."), which precedes the kissing of the altar, not vice versa, as in some diocesan uses and in early printed Roman Missals. The last Gospel (Jn 1:1–14), which was not yet in general use and is not included in early printed Roman Missals, is to be read at the altar rather than said in a low voice from memory as the celebrant returns to the sacristy (as was the practice in the Roman pontifical High Mass and in some diocesan uses). The rationale for this particular change may have been to focus on the meaning of the sacred text, and to avoid a perfunctory recitation.

The most significant innovation in Burchard's ordo concerns the reverential gesture for the consecrated Eucharist: when the celebrant has pronounced the dominical words over the bread, he is instructed to genuflect as a sign of adoration ("genuflexus eam adorat"). Then he elevates the consecrated Host, and after having placed it on the corporal again, he genuflects a second time. In the same manner, the Consecration of the chalice is followed by a genuflection before and after the elevation. The genuflection replaces the "medium bow" that is indicated in *Indutus planeta* for the adoration of the Body of the Lord. Until the later Middle Ages, bowing toward the consecrated species remained the priest's liturgical gesture of adoration, while kneeling in the presence of the sacrament was a characteristic expression of lay piety. The new practice was gaining ground in the late fifteenth and early sixteenth centuries. Burchard's ordo of 1502 systematically stipulates genuflections, not only for the double Consecration of bread and wine, but also in subsequent moments of the rite when a sign of reverence to the Body and Blood of Christ is called for (when the priest uncovers or covers the chalice with the pall, and when he takes the consecrated Host).

16

The Shape of the Tridentine Mass

The liturgical life of the late medieval Western Church was not in a general state of decay, but there were certainly aspects in need of correction. Early modern reformers denounced priests for signs of greed, a lack of preparation, carelessness in liturgical functions, or disregard for rubrics. Such grievances can be seen as part of a general critique of the state of the clergy, and appeals for moral renewal were widely shared at the time.

The profound rupture of the Protestant Reformation had a momentous impact on liturgical life. Martin Luther (1483–1546) rejected the sacrificial character of the Mass and condemned the Roman Canon. However, he changed the ritual structure of the Mass only gradually, and in many Lutheran church orders, some elements that had a popular appeal were retained, including eucharistic vestments and the elevation of the consecrated species.[1] Other Reformers, such as Huldrych Zwingli (1484–1531) in Zurich, as well as the compilers of the English Book of Common Prayer (especially in its second edition of

[1] See Helmut Hoping, *My Body Given for You: History and Theology of the Eucharist*, trans. Michael J. Miller (San Francisco: Ignatius Press, 2019), 223–35.

1552), went much further in their rejection of Catholic liturgical tradition.

The Council of Trent (1545–1563)

Calls for renewed liturgical discipline were already heard during the first period of the Council of Trent from December 1545 to March 1547. However, the question was resumed in earnest only in its last period, from January 1562 to December 1563, alongside the deliberations about the decree on the sacrifice of the Mass. The bishops and religious superiors representing various European nations at the council expressed a strong desire for a unified missal.[2] At the same time, it seems to have been the prevailing view among the Council Fathers that they were not in a position to undertake the revision of liturgical books themselves. In the final session on December 4, 1563, it was decided that several reform measures, which the council was not able to complete, should be left to the pope, among them the reform of the breviary and of the missal. The discussions among the Council Fathers served to establish two fundamental principles for this work: in the first place, the Council Fathers supported a unification of the Order of Mass and its rubrics; any celebration of Mass was meant to conform to this general standard. Second, there was a broad consensus that the Roman Rite should be pruned of more recent accretions, especially those

[2] See Hubert Jedin, "Das Konzil von Trient und die Reform des Römischen Meßbuches", *Liturgisches Leben* 6 (1939): 37–45, and Hubert Jedin, "Das Konzil von Trient und die Reform der liturgischen Bücher", *Ephemerides Liturgicae* 59 (1945): 28–30.

containing apocryphal material, those reflecting private devotions, and those judged to be superstitious.

The Missale Romanum of 1570

Following the publication of the *Breviarium Romanum* in 1568, the new edition of the *Missale Romanum* was promulgated by Pope Pius V with the bull *Quo primum* on July 14, 1570. The Ordinary of Mass (*Ordinarium Missae*) is largely indebted to Burchard's ordo of 1502 (except for the offertory procession, which was not included). Burchard's rubrical instructions are the main source for the *Ritus servandus in celebratione Missae* ("Rite to be observed in the celebration of Mass") that is placed at the beginning of the missal.

While liturgical books from the later Middle Ages contain a range of tropes—that is, texts (in both poetry and prose) added to embellish or augment chants from the Order or from the Proper of the Mass—the missal of 1570 explicitly proscribes the troping of the introit, the Kyrie, and the Gloria.

Considerable work was done on the liturgical calendar.[3] The very full sanctoral cycle of the pre-Tridentine books was substantially reduced, with the aim of bringing the temporal cycle to the fore again, especially in Lent. There were no significant alterations in the structure of the temporal cycle of the liturgical year, which had been established since the early Middle Ages, and few modifications

[3] For a concise overview, see Anthony Chadwick, "The Roman Missal of the Council of Trent", in *T&T Clark Companion to Liturgy*, ed. Alcuin Reid (London: Bloomsbury T&T Clark, 2016), 116–17.

were made in its prayers, chants, and readings. The most substantial change was the purging of the poetic sequences to be sung before the Gospel, except those for Easter, Pentecost, and Corpus Christi (as well as the Requiem Mass).

The Common of Saints was laid out more systematically, with complete Mass formularies. The number of votive Masses was reduced; their use was strictly regulated and restricted to weekday ferias.

The Shape of the Tridentine Mass

The *Missale Romanum* of Pius V thus stands in continuity with the plenary missals of the Roman Rite in the form used by the papal curia, which go back to the thirteenth century. This continuity extends even further to the time of the Gregorian reform in the eleventh century, and, in the essential structure and contents of the rite, to the papal stational Mass of *Ordo Romanus I*. Perhaps the most momentous novelty concerns the form of celebration. The *Ordinarium Missae* of 1570 contains some rubrical instructions for the Solemn, or High, Mass (*Missa solemnis*), with the assistance of deacon and subdeacon, as well as musical notation for the parts of the rite that are to be sung, including the intonations of the Gloria and Credo, the Prefaces, the Lord's Prayer, and the dismissal. However, the comprehensive and detailed *Ritus servandus* in the opening section of the missal seems to give priority to the Low Mass (*Missa lecta*), which was said (rather than sung) by a priest with the assistance of one or more servers. The indications for the Solemn Mass appear as additions to an underlying shape and structure, which is that of the Low Mass. Hence, it could be argued that the *Ritus servandus* ratifies the shift, which began with the Franciscan ordinal *Indutus planeta*, toward an understanding that the ritual forms of the Mass were, as Chadwick has aptly put it, "based on low Mass rather than low Mass being a reduction of the normative pontifical Mass, from which the solemn form with deacon and subdeacon is also a reduction".[4] There were practical reasons in favor of the Low Mass: above all, it was better suited to the demands of pastoral care, especially in the countryside, since it could be celebrated in places that lacked the human resources needed for the solemn liturgy. Furthermore, the simpler form of the Mass proved to be extremely useful in the worldwide missionary expansion of the Catholic Church in the early modern period. The sung liturgy was still cultivated, especially on important occasions of the Church's year, and the post-Tridentine period is distinguished by a thriving of sacred music. At the same time, the conceptual shift that can be observed in the 1570 missal reversed a liturgical principle that the solemn pontifical liturgy is the normative exemplar, in which all other celebrations of Mass participate to a greater or lesser degree. This principle had shaped the development of the Roman Mass since the late ancient and early medieval periods.

The increasing predominance of the simplified, spoken ritual meant that the sensory dimensions of the liturgy and hence the stimuli for the meditative and affective participation of the laity were curtailed. The structure of the Solemn Mass is not a linear sequence but rather a complex fabric of different ritual actions that are performed simultaneously. Paul Barnwell applies to this fabric the musical concept of "polytextuality"[5] and argues

[4] Ibid., 108–9.

[5] See Paul S. Barnwell, "The Nature of Late Medieval Worship: The Mass", in *Late Medieval Liturgies Enacted: The Experience of Worship in Cathedral and Parish Church*, ed. Sally Harper, Paul S. Barnwell, and Magnus Williamson (London and New York: Routledge, 2016), 216–18.

that it offered the laity various ways of engaging with it. As a result of the shift from ritual complexity toward the Low Mass, and the retention of almost exclusive use of Latin, the post-Tridentine period led to greater disparity between the "official" liturgy that was performed by the priest at the altar and the devotional exercises the laity used to follow it.

The Council of Trent's decision to leave the reform of the missal and breviary in the hands of the pope (and thus also his curia) inaugurated a period of unprecedented standardization of the Latin liturgical tradition. The medium of printing—now closely supervised by ecclesiastical authority—meant that uniform liturgical books could much more easily be produced and distributed throughout the Catholic Church. Thus, the sixteenth century marks a decisive moment in the long transformation from oral to written culture, with profound consequences for the celebration of the liturgy. The desire to strengthen the visible unity and cohesion of the Church, which had already been felt at Trent, led to the adoption of the Roman books even where an older tradition existed, with some notable exceptions that included the Ambrosian Rite in Milan and the Mozarabic Rite in Toledo. At the same time, the prevalence of a prescriptive liturgical book does not produce simple uniformity in the ways in which the liturgy is enacted, let alone experienced.

17

From the Tridentine Period to the Liturgical Movement

The publication of normative liturgical books for the Roman Rite in the decades after Trent included the *Pontificale Romanum* (1596) and the *Caeremoniale Episcoporum* (1600) for pontifical celebrations. The *Rituale Romanum* (1614) for all those sacraments and sacramentals not reserved to bishops was never imposed as such but was rather intended as a model to be adapted in local rituals. In 1588, Pope Sixtus V created the Sacred Congregation of Rites, which was to give authentic answers to questions arising from the new liturgical books and ensure the observance of liturgical norms. The minor changes and additions that subsequent popes made in the missal did not affect the basic structure and shape of Mass. Thus, the period between 1570 and the mid-twentieth century was marked by an extraordinary ritual stability. The English liturgist and historian Adrian Fortescue did not consider this liturgical centralization felicitous but conceded that it was widely considered necessary for the good of the Church at a time of crisis.[1] However, it should also be noted that in an increasingly global church, the Tridentine reforms

[1] Adrian Fortescue, *The Early Papacy to the Synod of Chalcedon in 451*, 4th ed., ed. Alcuin Reid (San Francisco: Ignatius Press, 2008), 36.

were applied in varying degrees and with different speeds. Local customs not only persisted but were purified and gained new vigor where dedicated pastors implemented the council's program of renewal effectively.

Questions of Liturgical Participation

The Protestant Reformers' emphasis on the royal priesthood of the baptized promoted conscious participation of the people in church services. Renaissance Humanism and the new technology of printing led to a focus on worship as text.[2] Consequently, participation was largely concerned with language comprehension, and the prevailing use of Latin in the Roman Rite came under severe criticism. At the Council of Trent, the question of liturgical language was debated with remarkable depth, and the arguments produced by the Protestant Reformers were considered very seriously.[3] The *Decree on the Sacrifice of the Mass* (1562) contains a carefully worded exposition on the subject, stating that it did not seem *expedient* to the Council Fathers that the Holy Mass should *generally* be celebrated in the vernacular. However, the Council Fathers recognized the value of the liturgical texts for the instruction of the faithful in a language that was intelligible to them. Therefore, pastors and those entrusted with the care of souls should preach frequently about what is read at Mass, especially on Sundays and feast days.[4]

[2] See Aidan Kavanagh, *On Liturgical Theology: The Hale Memorial Lectures of Seabury-Western Theological Seminary, 1981* (Collegeville, MN: Liturgical Press, 1984), 104, and John Bossy, *Christianity in the West, 1400–1700* (Oxford: Oxford University Press, 1985), 103.

[3] See H. A. P. Schmidt, *Liturgie et langue vulgaire: Le problème de la langue liturgique chez les premiers Réformateurs et au Concile de Trente*, Analecta Gregoriana 53 (Rome: Apud Aedes Unversitatis Gregorianae, 1950), 81–198.

[4] Council of Trent, Session 22 (September 17, 1562), *Decree on the Sacrifice of the Mass*, chapter 8; see also canon 9.

The festive culture of the Baroque period saw a great flourishing of sacred music, art, and architecture, which engaged the senses of the faithful and had the capacity of leading them to a profound understanding of the mysteries celebrated in the liturgy. Still, the perceived gap widened between the "clerical" liturgy performed by the sacred ministers in the sanctuary and the ways the laity found to participate in it. In the Catholic Enlightenment of the eighteenth century, efforts were made to promote the people's understanding of and partaking in the liturgy. There were demands to introduce the vernacular language, the celebration "facing the people", and, in general, to simplify rites in order to make them more intelligible. At the time, various currents in the Church endorsed similar ideas, though for different motives, such as Jansenism in France and Italy, which advocated a return to early Christian liturgical practice to instill a more restrained piety and seriousness in the moral life. Some of these demands were supported by the rationalist zeitgeist, which saw Christian worship above all as a useful exercise for the moral edification of the individual and for the building up of society. They also coincided with agitation for national churches under the patronage of the monarch and with greater independence from the papacy, as is evident by Josephism and Febronianism in the German-speaking lands.

The Liturgical Movement of the Nineteenth and Twentieth Centuries

The modern Liturgical Movement is connected with the rebirth of Benedictine monasticism after the devastations that the French Revolution and the Napoleonic wars brought to the Catholic Church in Europe. Prosper Guéranger (1805–1875), who refounded the Abbey of

Solesmes in France in 1832, made a stirring appeal in the first volume of his popular work *L'Année Liturgique* (*The Liturgical Year*), published in 1845: "Open your hearts, children of the Catholic Church, and come and pray the prayer of your Mother."[5] Thus, Guéranger stood at the beginning of a movement that aspired to make the unique spiritual treasure enshrined in the liturgical books of the Church more accessible to the ordinary faithful and place it at the heart of their devotional life.

A defining moment was Pope Pius X's motu proprio *Tra le sollecitudini* (originally written in Italian) on the restoration of church music (1903). The fundamental principle of *Tra le sollecitudini*, "active participation", was to become the cornerstone of liturgical renewal in the twentieth century:

> It being our ardent desire to see the true Christian spirit restored in every respect and preserved by all the faithful, we deem it necessary to provide before everything else for the sanctity and dignity of the temple, in which the faithful assemble for the object of acquiring this spirit from its indispensable fount, which is the active participation in the holy mysteries and in the public and solemn prayer of the Church.[6]

Much ink has been spilt on the interpretation of "active participation", and more recently, there have been valid attempts at a renewed reading of this principle, which gives priority to interior participation in the prayer and

[5] Cited in Cuthbert Johnson, *Prosper Guéranger (1805–1875): A Liturgical Theologian* (Rome: Studia Anselmiana, 1984), 350.

[6] Pius X, Motu Proprio on the Restoration of Sacred Music *Tra le sollecitudini* (November 22, 1903), English translation at https://adoremus.org/1903/11/tra-le-sollecitudini/.

sacrifice of Christ and his Church.[7] At the time, Pius X demanded new attention to the quality of liturgical celebrations, especially regarding sacred music, and a revision of liturgical books, which he began with a new edition of the breviary in 1911.

The Liturgical Movement, which flourished above all in French- and German-speaking countries in the first half of the twentieth century, intended to bring the people to a closer understanding and love of the rites of the Church. Thus, the Belgian Benedictine Lambert Beauduin (1873–1960), in a widely received paper at the 1909 Malines Catholic Congress, called for "a more enlightened and hierarchical piety" that was grounded in the liturgy itself.[8] To achieve this means, Beauduin proposed vernacular editions of the missal and other liturgical books for the use of the faithful, as well as liturgical periodicals and study weeks. Beauduin also recommended the dialogue Mass, in which the people would make the responses to the priest, rather than just the servers at the altar.

The short book *Vom Geist der Liturgie* (*On the Spirit of the Liturgy*), published in 1918 by Romano Guardini (1885–1968), a German theologian of Italian background, became a foundational text of the Liturgical Movement. Like Beauduin, Guardini wanted to introduce the ordinary faithful to the liturgy as "the supreme example of an objectively established rule of spiritual life".[9] At the same

[7] See, above all, Joseph Ratzinger, *The Spirit of the Liturgy*, trans. John Saward (San Francisco: Ignatius Press, 2000); also Daniel G. Van Slyke, "*Actuosa Participatio* from Pius X to Benedict XVI: Grace and Gregorian Chant", *Antiphon* 23 (2019): 101–44.

[8] Lambert Beauduin, "La vraie prière de l'Église", in *Dom Lambert Beauduin et le renouveau liturgique*, ed. André Haquin (Gembloux: Éditions Duculot, 1970), 241.

[9] Romano Guardini, *The Spirit of the Liturgy*, trans. Ada Lane (London: Sheed & Ward, 1935), 121.

time, however, Guardini and the Benedictine monks of Maria Laach in Germany gave the Liturgical Movement a new direction. While the texts and rubrics of the liturgical books were largely followed, changes were introduced to the form of celebration, with the idea of making the liturgy more approachable to the people of his time, such as Mass "facing the people" and vernacular hymns. Guardini also promoted the minimalist aesthetics that became widespread in sacred art and architecture. Bishops in various European countries were increasingly concerned about such tendencies.

While Pope Pius XII approved the principal aims of the Liturgical Movement in his encyclical on the sacred liturgy, *Mediator Dei* (1947), he rejected certain excesses of its protagonists and recalled the need to respect liturgical tradition. At the same time, Pius XII began a process of liturgical reform that culminated in the renewed Holy Week of 1955. Thus, the pope in many ways anticipated the Second Vatican Council.

18

The Second Vatican Council and the Reform of the Rite of Mass

The Constitution on the Sacred Liturgy, *Sacrosanctum concilium*, was the first document that came out of the Second Vatican Council. The Council Fathers approved it almost unanimously (2174 votes to 4), and Pope Paul VI promulgated it on December 4, 1963. According to Benedict XVI, who participated in the council as a theological expert, this was not just a pragmatic decision, since liturgy was a theme that seemed much less controversial than others; rather, beginning with divine worship reflected the right ordering of the Church's life and mission, and in particular "God's primacy, the absolute precedence of the theme of God.... When the focus on God is not decisive, everything else loses its orientation."[1]

Sacrosanctum concilium

The conciliar constitution clearly is a fruit of the Liturgical Movement, which had reached the height of its influence

[1] Benedict XVI, "On the Inaugural Volume of My Collected Works", in *Theology of the Liturgy: The Sacramental Foundation of Christian Existence*, vol. 11 of *Joseph Ratzinger Collected Works*, ed. Michael J. Miller, trans. John Saward and Kenneth Baker, S.J. (San Francisco: Ignatius Press, 2014), xv.

in middle decades of the twentieth century. Building on Pope Pius XII's encyclical *Mediator Dei*, the first chapter of *Sacrosanctum concilium* offers principles of liturgical theology as well as general and particular norms for liturgical reform. The council called for a general *instauratio* ("restoration" or "renewal") of the liturgy in order to communicate more clearly and effectively the graces signified in sacred signs. Those parts that are not of divine institution, but have grown through history, were to be ordered in such a way that both texts and rites would be more accessible and facilitate the full, active participation of the faithful.[2]

With a view to maintaining a balance between retaining "sound tradition" and allowing for "legitimate progress", the constitution called for a careful study of those parts of the liturgy that were to be "revised" (*recognoscendis*) (*SC* 23). Such a revision or review can include even substantial modifications but still has a limited scope.[3] This is certainly highlighted by *Sacrosanctum concilium*'s insistence that "there must be no innovations unless the good of the Church genuinely and certainly requires them; and care must be taken that any new forms adopted should in some way grow organically from forms already existing" (*SC* 23). However, the *Consilium* for Implementing the Council's Constitution on the Sacred Liturgy, which was established with Paul VI's motu proprio *Sacram liturgiam* of January 25, 1964, gave a maximalist reading of *recognitio*

[2] Vatican Council II, Constitution on the Sacred Liturgy *Sacrosanctum concilium* (December 4, 1963), no. 21, https://www.vatican.va/archive/hist_councils/ii_vatican_council/documents/vat-ii_const_19631204_sacrosanctum-concilium_en.html (hereafter cited in text as *SC*).

[3] See Pontifical Council for Legislative Texts, "Nota Esplicativa X: La natura giuridica e l'estensione della 'recognitio' della Santa Sede", *Communicationes* 38 (2006): 10–11.

and launched a thorough-going reworking of all the existing liturgical books of the Roman Rite.[4]

The Post-Conciliar Liturgical Reform

The overarching principle of reform, endorsing a key objective of the Liturgical Movement, was to promote "active participation" in the liturgy. The Council Fathers desired that the faithful should take part in the celebration of the liturgy "fully aware of what they are doing, actively engaged in the rite, and enriched by its effects" (*SC* 11). In the immediate post-conciliar period, this principle manifested itself especially in three concrete steps: (1) the full introduction of the vernacular for liturgical celebrations, (2) the simplification of rites, and (3) their adaptation to local cultures, above all, but not only, in mission territories.

The Sacred Congregation of Rites' instruction *Inter oecumenici* (September 26, 1964) introduced moderate changes in the *Ordo Missae*.[5] For instance, Psalm 42 was removed from the introductory rites, some prayers that used to be said in a low voice were now meant to be audible, including the doxology of the Canon of the Mass and the embolism after the Lord's Prayer. The structure and contents of the liturgical year largely remained the same.

[4] A firsthand account of the *Consilium*'s work is given by its long-term secretary, Annibale Bugnini, in his autobiographical book *The Reform of the Liturgy: 1948–1975*, trans. Mathew J. O'Connell (Collegeville, MN: Liturgical Press, 1990).

[5] Sacred Congregation of Rites, Instruction for the Right Implementation of the Constitution on the Sacred Liturgy *Inter oecumenici* (September 26, 1964), no. 48. The *editio typica* of the revised *Ordo Missae* was published on January 27, 1965; see *Notitiae* 1 (1965): 101–2.

The first of the "interim missals", as they have been called with hindsight, was published and implemented in the United States already on November 29, 1964 (the First Sunday of Advent). Contrary to the directives of the *Inter oecumenici*, this edition contained most of the texts that could be used in the vernacular only in English, not in Latin. The extensive use of English and the sweeping introduction of new altars where the priest was facing the people were experienced as a significant rupture in the liturgical life of the Catholic Church.[6]

Further changes were made to the Mass until the promulgation of the substantially altered *Ordo Missae* and the typical edition of the *Missale Romanum* of 1969/1970. While the Roman tradition had for many centuries used only one Eucharistic Prayer (*Canon Missae*), the number of Eucharistic Prayers was extended to four in the new Order of Mass, and several others have been added since.[7] There were significant changes in the "soft spots" of the Mass that had developed in the course of the medieval period (introductory, offertory, and concluding rites). The structure of the liturgical year was thoroughly reworked, including the removal of Pre-Lent (Septuagesimatide) and the Pentecost Octave. This was certainly the most extensive and thorough reform of the Roman Rite ever since its formative period in late antiquity. Going beyond the revision of liturgical books, the social and cultural transformations

[6] See the instructive articles by Susan Benofy in the *Adoremus Bulletin Online Edition*: "The Day the Mass Changed: How It Happened and Why—Part 1", February 15, 2010, https://adoremus.org/2010/02/the-day-the-mass-changed/, and "The Day the Mass Changed: How It Happened and Why—Part 2", March 15, 2010, https://adoremus.org/2010/03/the-day-the-mass-changed-how-it-happened-and-why-part-ii/.

[7] See the Eucharistic Prayers for Reconciliation and for Various Needs in the Appendix to the Order of Mass of the third typical edition of the Roman Missal, as well as the Eucharistic Prayers for Masses with Children.

of the 1960s also affected the ritual shape of the Mass: jazz, folk, and pop music found their ways into the liturgical celebration; historical patrimony was replaced with modern forms of artistic expression.

Loss and Gain

These profound changes have made the Mass more accessible to the faithful and have enabled them to be more actively and consciously involved in its celebration. The new liturgical books offer greater flexibility for the sacramental rites, which has been used with great profit in more recently evangelized cultures. The Roman Lectionary's three-year cycle for Sundays and two-year cycle for weekdays have enriched the use of Holy Scripture in the Mass, as envisaged by the Council Fathers (*SC* 24).

Along with real benefits, however, the extraordinarily rapid production and implementation of the new liturgical books and their many vernacular translations have created problems, which we now see more clearly at some historical distance. Joseph Ratzinger was himself formed by the Liturgical Movement and stated his conviction that "this new missal [of Paul VI] ... brought with it a real improvement and enrichment."[8] On the other hand, writing as pope, he spoke of "misunderstandings and errors in the practical implementation of the reform",[9] since "not infrequently ... 'active participation' has been confused with

[8]Joseph Ratzinger *Milestones: Memoirs 1927–1977*, trans. Erasmo Leiva-Merikakis (San Francisco: Ignatius Press, 1998), 148.

[9]Benedict XVI, Address to Participants in the Congress Promoted by the Pontifical Athenaeum of Saint Anselm on the 50th Anniversary of Foundation (May 6, 2011), https://www.vatican.va/content/benedict-xvi/en/speeches/2011/may/documents/hf_ben-xvi_spe_20110506_sant-anselmo.html.

external activity."[10] The focus on revising external forms has contributed to a self-contained notion of worship that does not transcend ordinary experience and is not transparent to the sacramental presence of Christ.

The delicate working of ritual was not sufficiently recognized in the liturgical reform, even where it was applied with the best intentions. Ritual as a system of symbolic communication is characterized by custom, rigor, and repetition. Hence, it gives the impression of being perennial, and it is precisely this stability that makes it work as ritual. Whether or not such claims are made explicitly, rites embody the traditions of the community that is formed by them. The at least tacit assumption of the liturgical reform was that ritual forms can easily be exchanged and replaced with their historical antecedents. However, such ritual change can have a lasting detrimental effect on the system of symbolic communication as such, by suggesting that ritual does not matter in the end.

[10] Benedict XVI, Video Message for the Closing of the 50th International Eucharistic Congress in Dublin (June 17, 2012), https://www.vatican.va/content/benedict-xvi/en/messages/pont-messages/2012/documents/hf_ben-xvi_mes_20120617_50cong-euc-dublino.html.

19

Ongoing Liturgical Renewal

As this brief historical overview has shown, liturgical life is never static. Even in the period of unprecedented standardization between the promulgation of the Tridentine Missal in 1570 and the mid-twentieth-century reforms, social, cultural, and artistic transformations shaped the actual celebration of Mass in a universal Church. As Joseph Ratzinger observed, "A liturgy in an Upper Bavarian village looks very different from High Mass in a French cathedral, which in turn seems quite unlike Mass in a southern Italian parish, and again that looks different from what you find in a mountain village in the Andes, and so on."[1] However, since "the most extensive renewal of the Roman Rite ever known",[2] elements of discontinuity and rupture with the liturgical tradition are undeniable, whether they are evaluated positively or negatively. The liturgy has in fact become a highly sensitive and controversial topic in the Church today. In this predicament, I will offer an outline of the different paths of ongoing

[1]Joseph Ratzinger, *The Spirit of the Liturgy*, trans. John Saward (San Francisco: Ignatius Press, 2000), 127.

[2]Benedict XVI, Video Message for the Closing of the 50th International Eucharistic Congress in Dublin (June 17, 2012), https://www.vatican.va/content/benedict-xvi/en/messages/pont-messages/2012/documents/hf_ben-xvi_mes_20120617_50cong-euc-dublino.html.

liturgical renewal indicated by Benedict XVI and his successor, Francis.

The Pontificate of Benedict XVI (2005–2013)

As a theologian and cardinal, Joseph Ratzinger wrote extensively on the liturgy and encouraged scholars and practitioners alike to articulate their unease about the present state of Catholic worship. He called for a "reform of the reform"[3] and a review of those elements that clearly disconnect contemporary practice from the received form of the Roman Rite, above all "the disappearance of Latin and the turning of the altars toward the people".[4] However, his election as pope confronted him with a dilemma, since he was keenly aware that liturgy cannot be constructed on a writing desk and authentic renewal "does not come about through regulation".[5] Hence, Benedict XVI did not take the initiative to introduce liturgical legislation to that effect, and there was no new *editio typica* of any liturgical book during his pontificate. Rather, he intended to resume the liturgical renewal desired by the council in a different key: "In a changed world, increasingly fixated on material things, we must learn to recognize anew the mysterious presence of the Risen Lord, which alone can give breadth and depth to our life."[6] The pontiff wanted to

[3] Joseph Ratzinger, "Assessment and Future Prospects", in *Theology of the Liturgy: The Sacramental Foundation of Christian Existence*, vol. 11 of *Joseph Ratzinger Collected Works*, ed. Michael J. Miller, trans. John Saward and Kenneth Baker, S.J. (San Francisco: Ignatius Press, 2014), 565.

[4] Joseph Ratzinger, foreword to *Turning Towards the Lord: Orientation in Liturgical Prayer*, by Uwe Michael Lang (San Francisco: Ignatius Press, 2004), quoted in *Theology of the Liturgy*, 393.

[5] Joseph Ratzinger, "Change and Permanence in Liturgy: Questions to Joseph Ratzinger", in *Theology of the Liturgy*, 521.

[6] Benedict XVI, Closing of the Eucharistic Congress in Dublin.

lead by example in his own celebrations—for instance, by extending the use of Latin, by placing a prominent crucifix in the center of the altar, and by distributing Holy Communion to the faithful kneeling and directly on the tongue.

At the same time, Benedict offered an important impulse in his momentous discourse to the Roman Curia on December 22, 2005, when he contrasted "a hermeneutic of discontinuity and rupture" in interpreting the Second Vatican Council with a "hermeneutic of reform", which he explained as "renewal in the continuity of the one subject [that is, the] Church which the Lord has given to us".[7] A key instance of such a renewal in continuity was the motu proprio *Summorum pontificum* of July 7, 2007, by which Benedict lifted previous restrictions on the use of the pre-conciliar liturgical books and made them into the "Extraordinary Form" of the Roman Rite, while the renewed liturgical books remain normative for its "Ordinary Form". These two usages of the one Roman Rite have sometimes been seen as manifestations of fundamentally different and, in the end, incompatible theological positions, especially regarding ecclesiology. However, the first article of *Summorum pontificum* explicitly rejects such an interpretation when it defines the two missals as expressions of the same *lex orandi* (rule of prayer) and hence of the same *lex credendi* (rule of faith).[8]

[7] Benedict XVI, Address to the Roman Curia Offering Them His Christmas Greetings (December 22, 2005), https://www.vatican.va/content/benedict-xvi/en/speeches/2005/december/documents/hf_ben_xvi_spe_20051222_roman-curia.html.

[8] Benedict XVI, Apostolic Letter Given Motu Proprio on the Use of the Roman Liturgy Prior to the Reform of 1970 *Summorum pontificum* (July 7, 2007), no. 1, https://www.vatican.va/content/benedict-xvi/en/motu_proprio/documents/hf_ben-xvi_motu-proprio_20070707_summorum-pontificum.html. The General Instruction of the Roman Missal (2002), no. 6, states that "the two Roman Missals [of 1570 and of 1970], although four centuries have intervened, embrace one and the same tradition."

Nonetheless, the phenomenological contrast between liturgical celebrations in the two usages make it appear difficult to speak of forms of the same rite. Such differences are less pronounced when, for instance, the Ordinary Form is celebrated in Latin and at an altar facing east instead of facing the people, but they still remain in the prayers and readings of the Mass, in many ritual elements, and in the structure of the liturgical year. In my reading, Benedict had in mind a slow and gradual process that was meant to begin with *Summorum pontificum*, which would eventually result in a "mutual enrichment" of the two forms.[9] At this point, it is also worth recalling the same Paschal Mystery is expressed in different, but by no means contrary or contradictory, ways in the Roman Rite, other Western rites (e.g., Ambrosian and Mozarabic), and in the many Eastern rites—and yet all of them have their place in the Catholic Church. The generous liturgical provision *Divine Worship* for the Personal Ordinariates for former Anglicans, created after Benedict's apostolic constitution *Anglicanorum coetibus* (November 4, 2009), would be another example of such legitimate diversity. The missal promulgated by his successor, Francis, in 2015 follows the essential structure of the Roman Rite, but at the same time enriches it with a "patrimony" that is partly derived from the wider medieval tradition (for instance, in the introductory and offertory rites) and partly derived from a characteristically Anglican style of prayer, brought into harmony with Catholic doctrine where necessary.

[9] Benedict XVI, Letter to the Bishops on the Occasion of the Publication of the Apostolic Letter "Motu Proprio Data" on the Use of the Roman Liturgy Prior to the Reform of 1970 *Summorum pontificum* (July 7, 2007), https://www.vatican.va/content/benedict-xvi/en/letters/2007/documents/hf_ben-xvi_let_20070707_lettera-vescovi.html.

The Pontificate of Francis (2013–)

Pope Francis did not focus on liturgical questions in the initial years of his reign. At the same time, he has made clear on many occasions that he sees the reforms of Vatican II as a fait accompli and there should be no going back. Thus, he called it mistaken to speak of a "reform of the reform".[10]

With his motu proprio *Magnum principium* of September 3, 2017, Francis largely placed the responsibility for translating the normative Latin liturgical books of the Roman Rite into the hands of bishops' conferences.[11] This decision substantially altered the provisions of the instruction *Liturgiam authenticam* of March 28, 2001, which gave the Holy See, through the Congregation for Divine Worship and the Discipline of the Sacraments, an active and leading role in the process. With *Liturgiam authenticam*, John Paul II had initiated, and Benedict XVI continued, a major revision of the post-conciliar translations of liturgical books, which brought fruit above all, but not only, in the English-speaking world.

The most significant decision of this pontificate in liturgical matters so far is the motu proprio *Traditionis custodes* of July 16, 2021, which not only abrogates the provisions of *Summorum pontificum* but also states that the post-conciliar liturgical books "are the unique [*unica*] expression of the *lex orandi* of the Roman Rite".[12] Francis has closely

[10] Gerard O'Connell, "Pope Francis: There Will Be No 'Reform of the Reform' of the Liturgy", *America: The Jesuit Review*, December 06, 2016, https://www.americamagazine.org/faith/2016/12/06/pope-francis-there-will-be-no-reform-reform-liturgy.

[11] See Maurizio Barba, "The Motu Proprio *Magnum Principium* on the Edition of Liturgical Books in the Vernacular Languages", *Antiphon* 21 (2017): 201–27.

[12] Francis, Apostolic Letter Issued "Motu Proprio" on the Use of the Roman Liturgy Prior to the Reform of 1970 *Traditionis custodes* (July 16, 2021), no. 1, https://www.vatican.va/content/francesco/en/motu_proprio/documents/20210716-motu-proprio-traditionis-custodes.html.

restricted the use of the 1962 missal under the centralized supervision of the Dicastery for Divine Worship and the Discipline of the Sacraments (as it is now called since the promulgation of the apostolic constitution *Praedicate evangelium* on March 19, 2022), with the clear intention that such use should gradually be phased out and the faithful attached to it should be brought to "a unitary form of celebration".[13] At the same time, it would appear that permission for the use of the pre-conciliar liturgical books is given generously for pastoral reasons, and the pope himself has decreed the Fraternity of Saint Peter exempt from *Traditionis custodes*.[14] If there is indeed a single expression of the "law of prayer" (and, by implication, of the "law of belief") in the Roman Rite, which is found only in the post-conciliar liturgical books, then there will be need for some clarification about the status of the older liturgical forms, which continue to be celebrated and nourish the spiritual lives of many faithful.

On June 29, 2022, Pope Francis published his apostolic letter on liturgical formation *Desiderio desideravi*. The document opens with a profound theological exposition that has much in common with the thought of Benedict XVI (even though he is not referenced), and the sections on liturgical formation contain many practical insights. While reiterating his conviction that "we cannot go back to that ritual form which the Council fathers, *cum Petro et sub Petro*, felt the need to reform", Francis calls for a rediscovery

[13] Francis, Letter to the Bishops that Accompanies the Apostolic Letter Motu Proprio Data *Traditionis custodes* (July 16, 2021), https://www.vatican.va/content/francesco/en/letters/2021/documents/20210716-lettera-vescovi-liturgia.html.

[14] "Decree of Pope Francis Confirming the Use of the 1962 Liturgical Books", February 11, 2022, available at https://www.fssp.org/en/decree-of-pope-francis-confirming-the-use-of-the-1962-liturgical-books/.

of "the richness of the general principles exposed in the first numbers of *Sacrosanctum Concilium*".[15] This teaching on the nature of the liturgy and its celebration commands the highest authority in a way that instructions for practical renewal, while binding on the Church, do not. Even if the concrete implementation of the conciliar constitution was overseen with the authority of holy popes, it does not engage the infallibility of the Church as in matters of faith and morals—neither does the liturgical reform of Saint Pius V after the Council of Trent. In an important contribution of 2003, Joseph Ratzinger argued that the framework set by the broad directives of *Sacrosanctum concilium* allows for "different realizations", and he cautioned: "Someone who does not think that everything in this reform turned out well and considers many things ... in need of revision is not therefore an opponent of the 'Council.'"[16] In the present moment, it would seem that Pope Francis's call to return to the general principles of *Sacrosanctum concilium* offers the best perspective for future directions of liturgical renewal.

[15] Francis, Apostolic Letter on the Liturgical Formation of the People of God *Desiderio desideravi* (June 29, 2022), no. 61, https://www.vatican.va/content/francesco/en/apost_letters/documents/20220629-lettera-ap-desiderio-desideravi.html.

[16] Joseph Ratzinger, "Fortieth Anniversary of the Constitution on the Sacred Liturgy: A Look Back and a Look Forward", in *Theology of the Liturgy*, 576.

20

Further Perspectives

In the preceding chapters, I have sketched the origins and development of the basic form and structure of the Mass in the Roman tradition. Looking back on a history that spans almost two millennia, I shall conclude by offering general considerations with a view to the present liturgical landscape.

Continuity and Change

Ever since the liturgical reforms that were initiated by Pope Pius XII in the mid-twentieth century, fully embraced by the Second Vatican Council (1962–1965) and implemented in the post-conciliar period, there has been an intense and often controversial debate on continuity and rupture in liturgical development. When this question is discussed, especially in online publications, the long and complex history of the Roman liturgy is not always sufficiently recognized. The trajectory I have traced shows both continuity and change. From its formative period in late antiquity, the ritual shape of the Roman Mass was affected by many religious, social, cultural, political, and economic transformations. But changes are to be expected over such a long period of time and over the wide geographical area where this rite has been used. It is the essential continuity that stands out.

Jesus instituted the Eucharist by means of his words and actions at the Last Supper, in anticipation of his redemptive self-offering on the Cross. The character of the Eucharist as an act of worship and of spiritual sacrifice emerges clearly in the early Christian period, even when sources are few and far between. Rooted in the Last Supper and formed by "Temple piety", the rite that stood as the heart of the Christian liturgy came to be celebrated as a memorial in which the sacrifice of Christ became present, and its saving effects were communicated to those who partook in it. Even in the modest material settings of the first two centuries, the sacred character of the Eucharist is evident in the place and time set apart for its celebration, and in the personal conduct expected from those who shared in it.

The Latin liturgical tradition becomes more tangible to us from the fourth century onward, above all with the early form of the Canon of the Mass attested by Ambrose of Milan around 390. The Roman Rite was forged in the practice of the papal stational liturgy of the late ancient and early medieval periods. Many sacramentaries of the Gregorian type begin with a separate section entitled "How the Roman Mass is to be celebrated", which corresponds to the essential structure of the solemn papal Mass of *Ordo Romanus I.* With the exception of "soft spots" (mainly in the introductory rites, the offertory, and the concluding rites), this Order of Mass remained remarkably stable in different liturgical settings (from magnificent cathedrals to modest rural chapels) and was codified in the post-Tridentine reform.

The further outward we move from this core structure, the more variety we find. Liturgical development always begins at the local level, and the Roman Mass became dominant in the Western Church through a long process that began in late antiquity, was accelerated by the Carolingian reforms in the eighth century, and reached a decisive point with the climax of the medieval papacy in the thirteenth century. At the same time, local and regional customs and traditions not only survived but were integrated into the Roman structure and thus enriched it. In response to the cataclysmic events of the Protestant Reformation, the bishops at the Council of Trent strongly supported a standardization of the Church's public worship. The Roman Missal of 1570 inaugurated a period of unprecedented stability in the celebration of Mass that would last until Vatican II. At the same time, however, there is always a certain measure of adaptation when a normative tradition is brought to life in a liturgical celebration. The ritual shape of the Mass will depend to a significant extent on the particular building, its material resources, and, last but not least, the persons involved. Each historical period put its stamp on the forms of the Church's public worship. The complex and varied world of modernity was bound to have such an impact as well.

Revisiting Liturgical Landmarks

As my brief overview has shown, some key landmarks of liturgical scholarship are in need of revision. Three areas in particular call for a renewed approach: First, recent contributions from various scholarly disciplines propose a fresh look at the Carolingian reforms and allow us to see in them an enrichment of the Roman tradition by the integration of Gallican elements. Second, in light of the wider manuscript evidence, the received typology of the early medieval *Ordo Missae* should be revisited. This would include a reconsideration of the role of private apology prayers in the Mass.

While some of these prayers are excessive in their length and penitential emphasis, they show an interiorization of priestly spirituality that continues to be valuable. After due pruning, these prayers were successfully integrated into the Roman Mass. Third, the liturgy of the later medieval period, which has sustained damning criticism from liturgical scholars, has been to some degree rehabilitated. This complex period offers not only signs of decay but also signs of vitality.

Taking a step further, it is high time to challenge the conventional narrative that the liturgy of the Western Church moved from early dynamic development through medieval decline to early modern stagnation and was only revived in the wake of Vatican II. This narrative still has considerable traction both in academic publications and in a wider public, despite its questionable hermeneutics—that is, the principles that guide the interpretation of historical sources. While recourse to Christian origins is evidently fundamental for Christian faith and worship, the attempt to canonize a supposedly classical form—whether it be the early liturgy before the Constantinian settlement in the fourth century, or the Roman Rite before the Carolingian reforms—does not do justice to the spiritual and cultural deepening that divine worship experienced in the long Middle Ages and also in the Baroque period. In a seminal contribution of 1966, Joseph Ratzinger brought to light the ambivalence of such liturgical purism that easily turns into unbridled desire for innovation. As he concluded pithily: "Mere archaism does not help and mere modernization even less."[1]

[1] Joseph Ratzinger, "Catholicism after the Council", *The Furrow* 18 (1967): 11. He renewed this critique in Joseph Ratzinger, *The Ratzinger Report: An Exclusive Interview on the State of the Church*, trans. Salvator Attanasio and Graham Harrison (San Francisco: Ignatius Press, 1985), 131–32, and Joseph Ratzinger, *The Spirit of the Liturgy*, trans. John Saward (San Francisco: Ignatius Press, 2000), 49–50, 52–56.

Joseph Ratzinger endorsed the idea of an "organic" development of the liturgy. By evoking the image of the pope as a "gardener" in his care for the liturgy, he contrasted a natural (or even botanical) model of growth with a technical model of constructing.[2] In the long history of the Roman Mass, there were no doubt moments of ritual change and innovation that make it difficult to apply the category "organic". From a wider perspective, however, I believe it is justified to see such substantial continuity once the Order of Mass acquired its distinctive structure in late antiquity, which was enshrined in the missal of 1570. Another factor should be considered here: premodern means of communication and administration meant that any liturgical reform preceded necessarily by a slow and gradual pace, and its application depended on local initiative. There is no precedence for the speed, the efficiency, and the global reach that marked ritual change since the Second Vatican Council.

This history is still being made and keeps taking unexpected turns. Hence, it would be unwise to make predictions for the future. The lockdowns prompted by the Covid crisis prevented countless people throughout the world from sacramental worship. The live-streamed and recorded services that proliferated in this dire situation made it possible for the faithful to listen to the Word of God and join in the prayer of the Church. At the same time, such practice obscures the true nature of what it means to "participate in" (or, to use an older expression,

[2] Joseph Ratzinger, "The Organic Development of the Liturgy", in *Theology of the Liturgy: The Sacramental Foundation of Christian Existence*, vol. 11 of *Joseph Ratzinger Collected Works*, ed. Michael J. Miller, trans. John Saward and Kenneth Baker, S.J. (San Francisco: Ignatius Press, 2014), 591.

"assist at") a liturgical celebration.[3] Given the revolutionary changes that have affected Western societies for a considerable time, we may note the remarkable persistence of the Roman liturgical tradition, its rediscovery among the younger generations of Catholics, and the attraction it still holds for a wider cultural public.

[3] It is worth recalling that different Catholic thinkers, such as Karl Rahner and Josef Pieper, objected to the introduction of televised Masses in the early 1950s; see Uwe Michael Lang, *Signs of the Holy One: Liturgy, Ritual, and the Expression of the Sacred* (San Francisco: Ignatius Press, 2015), 60–67.

GLOSSARY

This liturgical glossary explains technical terms related to the Roman Mass, which are used in this book. The list of terms is by no means exhaustive but is intended as a help for the reader.

active participation: Term introduced by Pope Pius X in 1903 to encourage a more attentive involvement of the laity in liturgical services. The Second Vatican Council made "fully conscious and active participation [*participatio actuosa*]" the main objective of its liturgical reform (*Sacrosanctum concilium* 14). Different interpretations have been given to this key principle, but it certainly includes interior participation by listening and silence as well as exterior participation through bodily postures and by joining in or responding to prayers.

altar: Sacred table in the sanctuary or chancel of a church on which the sacrifice of the Mass is offered and hence the most important liturgical object. Since the fourth century, altars have usually been made of stone and enclose the relic of a martyr or another saint.

ambo: Raised platform, lectern, or pulpit from which the readings from Holy Scripture are proclaimed. The ambo can also be the place of preaching. Monumental ambos from the medieval period are often placed in the nave of a church.

anamnesis: Greek term for "memory" or "remembrance" is used to indicate the act of remembering the Passion, death, and Resurrection of Jesus Christ in the celebration of the Eucharist, in obedience to his command at the Last Supper: "Do this in remembrance of me" (Lk 22:19; 1 Cor 11:24). More specifically, it denotes the section of the Eucharistic Prayer (see below), in which these saving events are recalled in connection with the act of offering.

anaphora: Greek term for "offering" used in Eastern Christian traditions in reference to the Eucharistic Prayer (see below).

basilica: An architectural term that describes a widely used type of Roman public building with a long, rectangular nave and a semicircular apse at the end. When Christianity was granted freedom in the Roman Empire in the early fourth century, this type of building was adopted for the construction of churches. The term "basilica" was used for the major churches of the city of Rome and later came to denote an honorary title the pope could bestow to churches throughout the world.

breviary: A liturgical book that contains all the texts needed for the recitation of the Divine Office (see below). The breviary developed in the high Middle Ages as a portable volume, while in a monastic or collegial setting, several books would be used for the daily offices.

Canon: In the Roman tradition, the Latin term originally meaning "measuring line" and used figuratively for "precept, rule". It came to be used for the Eucharistic Prayer (see below). The Canon of the Mass (*Canon Missae*) emerges first in the late fourth century and reaches its definitive form (except for minor modifications) in the pontificate of Gregory the Great (r. 590–604). Until the liturgical reform following Vatican II, it remained the single Eucharistic Prayer of the Roman Rite.

chant books: The sung texts for the celebration of Mass organized in a variety of liturgical books in the early medieval period. At first these books contained only texts, because melodies were transmitted by oral teaching and memorization. The

Proper chants of the Roman Mass came to be collected in the book known as the gradual, or Mass antiphoner. Books with a complete cycle of notated chants emerge around the year 900.

collect: The brief, variable opening prayer (*oratio* or *collecta*) said by the celebrant bishop or priest, which concludes the introductory rites (see below) of the Mass.

Common of Saints: Set Mass formularies for the liturgical celebration of saints that do not have proper texts appointed to them.

Communion rite: The section of the Mass that follows the Eucharistic Prayer (see below) and closes with the prayer after Communion. It contains the Lord's Prayer, the sign of peace, the fraction of the consecrated bread, and the distribution of Holy Communion. In the post–Vatican II missal, the Communion rite forms part of the Liturgy of the Eucharist (see below).

concluding rites: Consist of the blessing and dismissal of the people at the conclusion of Mass. In the Tridentine form of the Roman Rite, the dismissal precedes the final blessing and is followed by the reading of the last Gospel (Jn 1:1–14), which was added in the later Middle Ages.

Divine Office: The official daily prayer of the Church, which sanctifies particular hours of the day (canonical hours) and hence is also known as the Liturgy of the Hours (see also "breviary" above). The canonical hours consist above all of psalms, to which are added scriptural readings, hymns, and prayers.

doxology: A Greek term that literally means "a praising" and is used for a hymn or prayer of praise to God. The Eucharistic Prayer (see below) concludes with a Trinitarian doxology.

epiclesis: A Greek term that literally means "invocation" and specifically indicates the section of the Eucharistic Prayer (see below) where God the Father is asked to send the Holy Spirit to transform the offerings of bread and wine into the Body and Blood of Christ. The epicletic prayer *Quam oblationem* of the Roman Canon makes this petition without explicitly invoking the Holy Spirit. The epiclesis can also include an appeal for the spiritual fruits of sacramental Communion.

Eucharistic Prayer: The great prayer of "thanksgiving" (*eucharistia* in Greek) at the heart of the celebration of the Eucharist, also known in the Easter Christan traditions as "offering" (anaphora, see above), in which the offerings of bread and wine are consecrated as the Body and Blood of Christ.

facing east: The ancient Christian practice of turning toward the east (*ad orientem*) in liturgical prayer and in the layout of the apse of a church. The rising sun was understood as a symbol of the risen Christ and his Second Coming in glory. "Facing east" is commonly used to indicate the direction of prayer taken by priest and people together in the celebration of Mass.

Gregorian chant: The liturgical chant of the Roman church adapted and transformed in the Frankish realm beginning in the eighth century. The new chant idiom came to be known as "Gregorian", even though the ascription to Pope Gregory the Great is legendary. By the early thirteenth century, Gregorian chant was also used in the city of Rome.

Institution narrative: The actions and words Jesus Christ used at the Last Supper to institute the Eucharist. According to classical sacramental theology, the words of Christ pronounced by the priest consecrate the offerings of bread and wine and make them into the Body and Blood of Christ (see "Eucharistic Prayer" above).

intercessions: The section of the Eucharistic Prayer (see above) in which God the Father is petitioned on behalf of the living, including the Church's hierarchy, and the dead. The Roman Canon is unique in surrounding the Institution narrative with two distinct sets of intercessions, the first for the living, and the second for the dead.

introductory rites: The opening part of the Mass, generally including an entrance procession, a liturgical salutation, a penitential act, the Kyrie, the Gloria when appointed, and the collect. The introductory rites have undergone considerable development in the Roman tradition.

lectionary: A book specifying the scriptural readings for the celebration of the Mass or the Divine Office (see above). Originally, the Mass readings were indicated through marginal notes in biblical manuscripts, or through separate lists indicating their beginning and end. Later, the full texts were copied into separate manuscripts, which contained either the epistles (epistolatory) or the Gospels (evangelary) or combined all the readings into a single lectionary.

liturgy: From the Greek word *leitourgia*, originally meaning a public work or service for or on behalf of the people. In the Greek translation of the Hebrew Bible, it was chosen for the worship offered to God in the Temple of Jerusalem. In Catholic teaching, the liturgy is the solemn public worship of the Church for the glory of God's name and the sanctification of his people. This is understood above all as the work of the Blessed Trinity and an exercise of the eternal high priesthood of Jesus Christ, in which the whole Church as the communion of the faithful participates.

Liturgy of the Word/Liturgy of the Eucharist: The two main parts of the Mass in the post-Vatican II missal. The Liturgy of the Word follows the introductory rites (see above) and consists of the Scripture readings, the homily, the Creed (when appointed), and the universal prayer (or prayer of the faithful). The Liturgy of the Eucharist begins with the offertory rites (see below), has the Eucharistic Prayer (see above) at its center, and includes the Communion rite (see above).

Mass: From the word *missa*, which is related to *mittere* (to send) and gave the celebration of the Eucharist its name in the Western tradition. In the oldest available sources of the Roman Rite, the eucharistic liturgy concluded with "Ite, missa est" ("Go, this is the dismissal"). In the medieval period, the terms "Mass of the Catechumens" and "Mass of the Faithful" came to be used for two distinct parts of the rite. The origins of this use lie in the early Christian practice to dismiss catechumens (who were instructed for baptism), penitents, and others from the church before the offertory rites (see below). Only baptized faithful were allowed to participate in the eucharistic sacrifice.

missal: Sometimes also called "plenary missal". It contains all the texts required for the celebration of Mass in a single book (prayers, readings, chant texts). In the course of the Middle Ages, the missal replaced earlier types of liturgical books that were compiled for distinct liturgical actors—sacramentary (see below), lectionary (see above), and chant books (see above). The post-conciliar Roman Missal is not a plenary missal since it does not contain the scriptural readings.

offertory rites: Term derived from the Latin word *offerre*, "to offer"), and used for the liturgical actions of preparing the altar and placing on it the bread and wine for Consecration. The rite can include a procession with the eucharistic offerings and the use of incense. After preparing bread and wine, the priest washes his hands and says the prayer over the offerings.

Order of Mass (*Ordo Missae*): Set of invariable prayers (often supplied with musical notation) and ritual instructions (rubrics; see below) that instructs and directs the priest and other liturgical ministers how to celebrate Mass. As a distinct liturgical genre, the *Ordo Missae* emerged in the early medieval period. In the thirteenth century, it was incorporated into the missal of the Roman Curia.

Ordinary (of the Mass): Invariable texts of the Mass. In particular, the term is used to denote the Ordinary chants: Kyrie,

Gloria, Credo, Sanctus-Benedictus, and Agnus Dei. The Gloria and Credo are sung or said only on Sundays and feast days of a certain rank.

Ordines Romani: The name given to a collection of manuscripts that offer ritual descriptions and serve as practical instructions for actors in a variety of liturgical celebrations, including Mass, the Divine Office (see above), baptism, and ordinations. Of particular importance is *Ordo Romanus I*, which contains a detailed account for the pope's solemn stational liturgy (see below) in Easter week. Frankish liturgists adapted *Ordo Romanus I* as the standard and measure of the celebration of Mass to the local conditions and customs of their cathedrals and churches.

pontifical: A liturgical book containing the rites and ceremonies that are usually reserved to a bishop (from Latin word *pontifex* meaning "high priest", which was adopted for a bishop in Christian use), such as ordinations and dedication of churches.

Preface: Originally considered the beginning of the Eucharistic Prayer (see above). It offers praise and thanksgiving to God for a particular liturgical season or feast day. It begins with an introductory dialogue, contains a proper and variable part, and introduces the Sanctus.

private Mass: The celebration of Mass with only one or two assistants in the early medieval period, which spread first in monasteries and then among the secular clergy. In a "private Mass" (the term is infelicitous since every celebration of Mass is an action of the Church), the parts assigned in its solemn form to distinct liturgical ministries were recited by the priest himself, and they were increasingly spoken rather than chanted. As the space on side altars was smaller, the ceremonial was reduced and eventually the lessons were read by the priest at the altar.

Proper (of the Mass): The variable texts of the Mass that are assigned to a particular day in the liturgical calendar. In particular, the term is used for the Proper chants, which serve to accompany and elucidate the meaning of a specific ritual (introit, offertory, Communion), or a meditation on the Word of God (gradual, alleluia, or tract).

rite: When speaking of the Roman Rite or Byzantine Rite, a term understood as a coherent body of liturgical forms and ordinances that are followed by local churches within a particular territory. The Roman Rite originated in the city of Rome, was gradually adopted in the Western Church, and today is by far the most widely used among the liturgical rites of the Catholic Church.

rubrics: Instructions for the performance of a liturgical rite. With the development of the Order of Mass (see above), such instructions were included in liturgical books. Since they were usually written in red ink, they came to be known as rubrics (from *ruber*, the Latin word for "red").

sacramentary: The book containing the texts recited or chanted by the bishop or priest officiating at the celebration of Mass and other rites. In the early medieval Roman tradition, two types of sacramentaries have been identified: The Gelasian Sacramentary is believed to have been compiled originally for the use of priests in the city's titular churches. The Gregorian Sacramentary emerged from the collection of Mass books for the use of the pope when he celebrated at the Lateran (his cathedral) and in the stational churches of the city.

sacristy: The room in a church where vestments, sacred vessels and other liturgical furnishings are kept. It is the place where preparations for liturgical services are made and where the sacred ministers usually vest.

sanctoral cycle: Runs through the liturgical year in parallel with the temporal cycle (see below) and consists of the annual celebrations of the saints, with special honor given to the Blessed Virgin Mary.

schola cantorum: A formally structured association of trained singers in clerical orders in Rome who sang especially at papal liturgical celebrations. As a professional body and well-organized choir school, the Roman schola cantorum was probably founded in the late seventh century.

stational liturgy: When the pope (or his delegate) would celebrate Mass on appointed days during the liturgical year, and especially during Lent. Stational liturgies flourished in the early medieval period in the early medieval period. A particular church of the city (*statio*, literally, "station" or "position") was assigned for a given day, and the pope would move in solemn procession from his residence in the Lateran Palace to the stational church to celebrate Mass.

temporal cycle: Runs through the liturgical year in parallel with the sanctoral cycle (see above) and unfolds the mysteries of Christ from his Incarnation and Nativity through his Passion, death, Resurrection, and Ascension, to Pentecost and the expectation of his Second Coming.

RECOMMENDED READING

This book has attempted a broad overview of its topic. For a detailed history of basic structure and ritual shape of the Roman Mass that concludes with the aftermath of the Council of Trent, see Uwe Michael Lang, *The Roman Mass: From Early Christian Origins to Tridentine Reform* (Cambridge: Cambridge University Press, 2022).

The seminal work of Josef Andreas Jungmann, *The Mass of the Roman Rite: Its Origins and Development (Missarum Sollemnia)*, trans. Francis A. Brunner, 2 vols. (New York: Benziger, 1951–1955), is still valuable for its command of primary sources, even though Jungmann's narrative of decline from the original and pure idea of *eucharistia* needs to be questioned.

There are reference works that introduce the reader to liturgical sources, above all by Cyrille Vogel, *Medieval Liturgy: An Introduction to the Sources*, rev. and trans. William G. Storey and Niels Krogh Rasmussen (Washington, DC: Pastoral Press, 1981), and Éric Palazzo, *A History of Liturgical Books from the Beginning to the Thirteenth Century*, trans. Madeleine Beaumont (Collegeville, MN: Liturgical Press, 1993).

Among more recent works, Bryan D. Spinks, *Do This in Remembrance of Me: The Eucharist from the Early Church to the Present Day*, SCM Studies in Worship and Liturgy (London: SCM Press, 2013), is particularly strong on the eucharistic liturgy in the early Christian period and includes a survey of Eastern liturgical traditions, as well as Protestant communion rites. Helmut Hoping, *My Body Given for You: History and Theology of the Eucharist*, trans. Michael J. Miller (San Francisco: Ignatius Press, 2019), is indispensable for its theological depth and takes the narrative up to the present day.